FEARLESS MINDSET

FEARLESS MINDSET

A **LIFE-CHANGING BOOK** THAT WILL HELP YOU TAKE CONTROL OF YOUR **FEARS!**

BY

KURT GASSNER

Fearless Mindset
Kurt Gassner

Impressum
My-mindguide – The publishing trademarke of trendguide Capital GmbH, Klenzestr. 42a, 80469 Munich, Germany.

Reg. Nr. HRB Munich 206639, VAT 152 123 159, CEO: Kurt Friedrich Gassner
Web: www.my-mindguide.com, mail: gassner@my-mindguide.com

Paperback ISBN: 978-3-98793-922-8
Hardback ISBN: 978-3-98793-022-5

TABLE OF CONTENTS

WHY THIS BOOK CAN IMPROVE YOUR LIFE

The concepts of fear and danger are diametrically opposed. While danger is a circumstance that poses a risk of bodily harm or suffering, fear is a mental state that causes worry.

Fear raises plenty of questions in the mind at once. What exactly is fear? Is it a necessary emotion? Is it really so important to live a life free of fear?

Fear has a powerful existence in our lives, but asking to live without it may seem like too much to handle. The purpose of fear is to help us be guided effectively in the direction we ought to be headed. Fear is a protective measure of the mind and body against any harm that comes from within and outside forces. We have evolved to continue to enhance our features similarly to our ancestors, especially in high-quality weaponry such as strength or agility.

You fear what you don't understand. Fear is defined as an unpleasant emotional response to anticipation or awareness of a real or imagined threat. Everyone experiences fear to some degree, but you can learn how to be fearless with this inspiring book. This book shows you how to harness the power of fear and use it for good. Fear can make you stronger, but when controlled, it will allow you to achieve even more than you ever would have without it. Practice positive living and good deeds and be rewarded with a positive lifestyle!

And all of our body language, education, habits, behavioral features, differences, habits, qualifications, job titles, and positions make up our identity. Fear, on the other hand, may appear to be a necessary emotion at times, as long as it remains balanced and within our control.

Fear can be a useful tool as long as it doesn't rule our decisions or sabotage our efforts to make positive changes. Fear also serves as an instinctual protective mechanism, preventing us from engaging in the kind of careless and irresponsible behavior that the human race is known for.

The power is in your hands. Fearlessness is an action, not a feeling. It is a result of a well-thought-out process for purifying the mind. It is an attitude that you build within yourself by understanding what fear is and how it works. Within the next four weeks, you will learn how to see through the illusion that fear creates and begin to liberate yourself from what paralyzes your happiness and ability to grow.

To become fearless, one must first become powerful. You should be fearless in your approach to life's obstacles. Do not flee, and do not, under any circumstances, submit to injustice or wrongdoing. Continue to improve your self-power with the help of this book.

Expect the reciprocal power of goodness to repay your kindness. You may not notice the results right away, but they will come. Charity, positive thoughts, and good deeds accumulate excellent karmic wealth that you can bank on when the chips are down.

EXIT
FEARS

My-mindguide.com

WHAT IS FEAR?

Fear is the body's inherent alarm mechanism in response to a perceived immediate threat. It involves your physiological reactions to messages flooding your brain (heart palpitations, sweaty hands, shallow breathing) (you're in danger of being eaten, hit, embarrassed, falling, or failing). Even when you don't want it to, fear may quickly establish a loop that stimulates the fight or flight reaction.

We can create a connection with fear by perceiving it as information; we can then have a discussion with it.

We all have our own fears, whether it's the fear of rejection, failure, or any other form of fear, but in order to achieve something in this world and safeguard our self-esteem, we must learn to overcome fear and not be trapped by it.

Fear is suffering that you're trying to escape; for example, if you're afraid of public speaking, it suggests that there's something terrible about that experience that you're trying to avoid; it could be the possibility that people will judge you poorly or something else entirely. If you're afraid of rejection, your fear indicates that you think it'll be too painful to go through, and so on.

Now, in order to conquer fear, we must create even more fear! You must be more afraid of what will happen if you don't do that thing than of what will happen if you do it. It's as simple as that. For example, if you fear rejection, you should consider the fact that you will die alone, never develop your personality, and never seize opportunities. If and when you fear that more than the fear of rejection itself, you'll be equipped to move forward.

We cannot eliminate all fear from our lives in order to be happy. When we're actually in danger, we need to know. Being fearless occurs when we can recognize whether our fears are serving us, and if they aren't, we can work with them until we can bravely move forward.

Most of us haven't spent much time honing mental skills that protect us from the crushing impacts of self-doubt.

What if we understood exactly what we wanted to accomplish, had a plan to accomplish it, and never let bad feelings or self-defeating beliefs stop us from doing what we needed to do to reach our goals? Would we ever fail to reach our goals?

When we've removed the hurdles that keep us from realizing our full potential, we can acquire a fearless mentality. This is accomplished by learning to accept both what we have control over and what we do not. Once we grasp what is and isn't our duty, we can focus all of our attention on mastering the areas over which we have direct control, rather than wasting it on matters over which we have no control.

Guilt and fear are the two most common sources of squandered energy.

Guilt: Allowing our brains to focus too much on the past interferes with our capacity to live in the moment and appreciate the realities of life.

Fear arises when we pay attention to what might or might not happen in the future. Our focus is drawn away from the present moment once more, reducing our ability to make sound decisions.

There is only action in the moment. Fear arises only when we allow our imaginations to worry about the future. We should focus on the here and now in the hopes that whatever we improve in the short term will benefit us in the long run.

When we expect outcomes that are beyond our immediate control, we are setting ourselves up for failure. For example, how enjoyable is it to work for a boss who rates our performance based on circumstances over which we have no control?

High-Efficiency

To attain our full potential, we have to quit battling with ourselves and channel our energy into completing whatever goal we set for ourselves.

Inherited abilities can guide us in the right route. High performance, on the other hand, is earned rather than granted.

Any work that is completed properly—when those aspects under our direct responsibility are controlled and mastered; when we are completely at one with ourselves—is considered high-performance.

Practice with Intention

Deliberate practice is defined as any activity that accomplishes the following goals:

1. **Is specifically designed to improve performance** – It's vital to aim our mental resources toward goals over which we

have direct control, which boosts confidence and feelings of power. Directing our mental energy toward goals over which we have no direct control (e.g., "I have to win today"), on the other hand, considerably increases tension and causes emotions of powerlessness.

2. **Strives for goals that are just beyond one's degree of competence** – We must always strive for goals that are just a little bit out of reach so we believe they are attainable. It simply promotes thoughts and feelings of powerlessness if our goal is too far beyond our reach or ability level. This is why so many people fail to keep their New Year's resolutions.

3. **Provides feedback on results** – We need to track our progress in order to improve our abilities and confidence, and feedback empowers people to take charge of their own development. Feedback is utilized to determine which skill sets are helping to increase performance and which skill sets need to be isolated for further improvement.

4. **Requires a lot of repetition** – We need to isolate skills and practice them repeatedly until we master them.

Deliberate practice, for example, isn't simply striking a bucket of tennis balls with no specific goal in mind. Deliberate practice is hitting twenty slice serves with the goal of placing the ball within two feet of the target 80 percent of the time, constantly observing results and making needed adjustments, and doing so on a daily basis.

Mediocrity

Excuses and alibis keep us from taking responsibility and being accountable. Sure, it's human nature to blame others, but there's no way to get anywhere if you keep continuing down that path. It's just a road.

—Bennett, Wayne

What happens if we don't follow our dreams?

The majority of individuals do not give their dreams a chance. People talk about doing something, but few actually do it. Few people make even a smidgeon of an effort to make their goals a reality. Others give it a half-hearted effort before abandoning it in favor of safer, more convenient pursuits. However, research shows that those who do give it a shot end up being high performers as a result of their endurance over time.

Why do so many of us succumb to the mediocrity trap? Why do so many of us accept mediocrity?

Fear, as well as doubt and confusion inside oneself, are significant components – we inadvertently build a scared mind and settle for what is safe and simple rather than pursuing our aspirations.

Don't get too attached to the idea that dreams will never change; we must have the bravery to adapt to our goals.

THE ANATOMY OF FEAR

It's this four-letter word that wields so much power over our lives that we've come to accept it as a natural part of life. Fear pulls us away from what we really want, makes us feel unworthy, makes us feel weak, and most importantly, it makes us forget who we are.

But what if I told you that fear is all a figment of your imagination? Our mind fabricates a falsehood to keep us safe. What if I also told you that instead of dreading fear, embracing it as a friend could be one of the most effective methods to defeat the Goliath that dwells within each of us?

But first, let's look at how fear works to see why it's an essential illusion. Except for the fear of heights, which we develop within our first six months of life, and the fear of separation, most of our anxieties are learned through a process known as fear conditioning.

Some individuals are afraid of dogs, while others consider them to be family. When we experience a traumatic incident in our lives, the amygdala records it and generates a fear reaction the next time we encounter a situation similar to the trauma. By coupling the presence of a rat with unpleasant stimuli such as loud noises, a classic study conducted by John Watson in the 1920s taught a child to dread white rats. The baby immediately learned to be afraid of rats and other hairy animals. When the subjects were confronted with similar conditions, the amygdala still connected the events with a real threat, these fear responses were documented decades later.

In another fascinating study, lab monkeys that had never been exposed to snakes showed no fear of them when brought into touch with them for the first time. The lab monkeys, on the other hand, showed a greater dread of the same snakes in a second trial after seeing footage of their wild counterparts' terror responses when exposed to snakes.

This process, known as fear transference, shows that a first-hand experience is not required for a fear reaction to emerge; it can become our own simply by seeing others go through it. Most of our anxieties, according to this research, are acquired and/or transferred from previous experiences that our basic reptilian brain, the amygdala, immediately assimilate as true concerns.

Thinking of something as hazardous increases your chances of experiencing the fear responses connected with it, and thinking to the contrary reduces the hold that fear can have on you when you're doing something dangerous or out of your comfort zone.

Let's look at the many sorts of fear now that we've covered how fear works. Fear, in my opinion, can be classified; thus, I've divided fears into three categories: evolutionary fear, societal dread, and identity fear. This is my personal take on fear and ought to be regarded as food for thought.

1. The Fear of Evolution

We have hard-wired evolutionary fears that help us to escape pain and danger. When confronted with life-threatening events, our dread of pain and danger keeps us alive. Our forefathers in the African grasslands feared the threat posed by Sabre-toothed tigers, and this terror drove them to seek safety. The fear of danger and suffering were real fears that kept our forefathers alive in an unforgiving environment. They are still applicable today, allowing us to navigate the perils of modern society.

2. Societal Fears

The next type of dread is societal fear, which we learn at a young age through a process known as environmental conditioning. Worries of failure, embarrassment, and rejection are common cultural fears. We are exposed to situations as youngsters that instill these fears in us. For example, a humiliating experience might instill fears of disgrace and rejection, whereas a perceived sense of overachievement can instill fears of failure.

They don't have to be our own experiences; they may be someone else's, and as previously said, the primitive region of our brain, the amygdala, may store these traumatic events as our own, resulting in our deeply ingrained fear responses.

These worries arise as a result of occurrences outside of our control over which we have no influence, but our brains learn to make sense of them and generate fears that cause us to behave in the same manner we did when the incident first occurred.

3. Anxiety about One's Identity

Loneliness, lack of power, and ambiguity are common identity worries. These fears are powerful because they're at the core of who we are. Because we view our actions to have the worst possible outcomes, these worries can paralyze us into inaction.

Almost everything we do is designed to provide us a sense of security and belonging, allowing us to experience love on a communal as well as a more personal level. A danger to these most basic of human requirements can arouse our deepest concerns.

The majority of these worries, however, are not genuine; they are created and exaggerated by our subconscious mind. To keep us safe from the dangers our subconscious mind believes we can encounter, it creates a fear response, which most of us refer to as our "comfort zone."

Fear thrives in the dark, lonely areas of your comfort zone; fear, on the other hand, cannot exist in the vibrant pulse of adventure and the pursuit of your ambitions, for that is where bravery lives and magic happens.

The Fear Psychology

Despite the fact that psychologists have defined fear as an emotion, it is a very basic human emotion that can be compared to a simple feeling. Indeed, if emotions are made up of feelings and bodily reactions, fear would be the primary feeling component of anxiety or phobias, according to the psychology of emotions. Fear is something I prefer to refer to as a feeling rather than an emotion, and to explain why, it's vital to understand the difference between feelings and emotions in psychology. This distinction is currently unclear, and psychologists rarely make a clear distinction between feeling and emotion.

Emotions are multi-dimensional mental and physical processes that include both mental and physical components, such as feelings and physiological reactions. As a result, emotion is incomplete without feeling. Fear, which may or may not involve bodily reactions, can be both a sensation and an emotion because the simple feeling is purely psychological and doesn't involve bodily reactions. A student's fear at the test center, for example, would be accompanied by bodily reactions such as rapid heartbeat, heated face, dilated pupils, and so on. Although fear, which can have a feeling component, can be extremely simple and generic—even unconscious without a bodily reaction—it's not as powerful as anxiety, which must involve bodily reactions. Thus, if you are on stage performing a play, you may not directly detect any bodily reaction and may appear calm and normal, yet you may still experience fear and uneasiness.

Fear might thus be both a feeling and an emotion, but fear as a completely subjective or mental feeling component would be difficult to identify because it wouldn't be accompanied by observable or detectable physical reactions like fear as an emotion would. Anxiety, on the other hand, is an interior feeling that arises from a perceived threat rather than fear, which is triggered by external stimuli. Fear can be characterized as a conscious or unconscious externalized emotion or internalized feeling that may or may not be accompanied by bodily reactions.

Fear as an emotion and fear as a feeling, fear as conscious and fear as unconscious, fear with bodily reactions and fear without physiological reactions, fear in anxiety and fear in phobias—all of these nuances would all be distinguished in a psychology of fear. It's crucial to comprehend why fear happens and what bodily reactions occur when fear is a strong conscious emotion, as well as how this differs from fear as a feeling, which may or may not have bodily reactions and may or may not be conscious but is more likely unconscious.

For example, if you have an unconscious dread of old rundown buildings and you frequently dream of events in such houses, the dream may produce some bodily reactions, but it isn't obvious that the fear is producing the reaction. In this situation, the dread is just unconscious, and a feeling that develops in dreams, with the dreams being linked to body reactions rather than the terror. As a result, fear is a sensation rather than an emotion in this case. Some psychologists argue that this "fear" could simply be undefined anxiety, but since the reason for the fear (or anxiety, as they call it) is a fear of haunted houses, this is still an externalized fear and not an internalized anxiety. Fear, whether it be a sense or an emotion, is thereby externalized.

The distinction between feelings and emotions is akin to attempting to distinguish between meteoroids and asteroids in outer space, and it would necessitate a thorough examination of the mind's layers. At this time, there are insufficient frameworks or scientific evidence to make this distinction simple. The topic of emotion has, however, been the subject of recent investigations into consciousness. This subjective sensation of "what it's like to be" is particularly significant, as Thomas Nagel underlined in his classic work *What is it like to Be a Bat?* The subjective aspects of emotions are all important in the study of consciousness, and while hardcore physicalists who believe that our minds are nothing more than neuronal firings would dismiss the fact that an emotion has a feeling component, consciousness-focused studies have indicated that feeling, or the subjective aspect of being, is at the core of being human.

However, because the issue concerns the psychology of fear, it is critical to comprehend why fear occurs and what treatment options exist for fear. Fear can be described as an unconscious feeling of dread, or it might be a more complicated emotion like anxiety or externalized fear. Phobias, which are persistent pathological fears directed toward specific items and circumstances, are another type of fear. Phobias, such as a fear of spiders or heights, are exaggerated or intense kinds of fear that cause significant physical reactions, bordering on paranoia. Thus, fear can manifest as acute emotions with body reactions, such as worries or full-blown phobias; nevertheless, fear can just be a general feeling. To comprehend why fear occurs, we must first distinguish between the many types of dread:

- Fear as Emotions: Fear is a powerful emotional response to a situation, an object, or an event when it is accompanied by body reactions. Fear would naturally begin with a feeling or a subjective component because the sense of fear is internalized. This indicates that the person would 'feel' terrified of the circumstance before reacting to it. This type of fear, in which the individual is aware of the emotion and reacts strongly to it, is typically an emotional response, and hence manifests as a powerful emotion.

- Fear as a Sensation: Fear might simply manifest as a subjective feeling, a sense of unease, or an unconscious impression of danger or threat that does not elicit significant bodily responses. Fear is thus involuntarily released as an emotion in nightmares, slips of the tongue, lapses of focus, and so on.

- Fear as Anxiety: When internalized and even unexplained anxiety has a broad feeling of fear, fear as a feeling could be the subjective basis of anxiety. Anxiety starts with a fear, but it's often unconscious, internalized, and more widespread. Anxiety, on the other hand, has specific bodily reactions, which is how it varies from fear as an emotion.

- Fear as Phobias: Fear as phobias is a pathological emotional response to specific items or experiences that persists over time. The distinction between anxiety and phobia is that phobias are always externalized, whereas anxiety is internalized, and fear, whether externalized as an emotion or internalized as a feeling, is a component of both anxiety and phobias. Phobias, on the other hand, are abnormal responses to fear as a complicated emotion and body reaction. Because phobias are made up of emotions and powerful reactions, the reactions are magnified in phobias, causing people with phobias to respond in extreme ways and suffer panic attacks, especially owing to the intense and uncontrollable body reactions.

Understanding the origins of fear will be required in psychological therapeutic therapy, and this can be accomplished through neurological investigations and studies of physical reactions and mental states. Fear should be characterized in certain settings as basic sentiments or complicated emotional responses, and extensive fear could be examined in anxiety and phobia.

FEAR FACTOR

So, you've assessed your goals and selected the kind of life you want to live. You can picture it in your head, but something keeps getting in the way. Is it possible that it's fear?

Fear has a way of putting psychological pollutants into our minds that prevent us from achieving our objectives. Despite the fact that the terror is only perceived, it appears to be quite real. This phantom terror plays mind games with us, robbing us of any sensible thinking we need to keep moving forward.

When fear is felt, the fear-related part of the brain instinctively reacts. It causes symptoms including a beating heart, anxiousness, and sweaty hands. If your dread is based on questions about your own capacity, it will allow you to make an excuse for not being able to complete your assignment.

Fear is a completely unconscious process. You are compelled to think, believe, and behave in response to the terror you initially felt. If the apparent fear is based on negative past experiences, the subconscious mind will instill even more uncertainty, leaving you immovable, immobilized, and unable to take even the first step.

Because we do everything we can to avoid suffering or discomfort in our lives, we succumb to the concerns that our subconscious feeds us. This apprehension inhibits you from making the first move. Your ambition may throb within you at times, motivating you to take the next step, but the discomforts and doubts generated by fear can be so much stronger than your own ambitions that you are unable to follow through.

This worry eats away at your self-assurance over time. You start making excuses because you can't get things done. You take on the role of the victim. You wallow in self-pity. You start to feel down. All in the name of dread, your self-esteem plummets.

Fear Eats Away at One's Self-Esteem

Have you ever noticed how easy it is for you to come up with fantastic, profitable ideas? You're certain this is the big one, the granddaddy of all ideas. Your sense of excitement rises the instant you come up with an idea. You can't wait to tell your friends and family about it. However, as time passes, the enthusiasm fades.

People in your life have heard it so many times that they're just politely listening to your hype. You start to gain a reputation for being "all talk and no action." Your self-assurance gradually erodes. How many times has something like this happened to you before? What factors do you believe have a role in this syndrome? Is it possible that it's fear?

You must cope with the fear component in your life in order to cross the bridge from aspiration to accomplishing your goals. You may be brave in other parts of your life, but there is always something working against you when it comes to achieving your goals. Fear is that something.

When fear gets in the way of your strategy, it jeopardizes your ability to carry it through. Your enthusiasm fades over time, and everything comes to a halt. You're disappointed in yourself once more, unsure of what happened. Your self-assurance plummets dramatically. You withdraw out of shame. Your self-esteem plummets. You stay in hibernation until you feel safe enough to come out again, hoping no one asks about your latest failed effort.

Success-Related Phobias

Fear takes control of your life once it has eroded your self-confidence. It lurks in the subconscious and controls your very existence. Each poor attempt or avoidance of something due to fear reinforces the frightened behavior even more. This fear then spreads to every aspect of your existence. Your self-esteem suffers as a result of the loss of self-confidence. As one begins to experience what many refer to as the "fear of success," the self-critic dominates one's cognitive process, and self-doubt ultimately creeps in. If you don't face your fear, it will continue to ruin your every move.

Let's look at what the fear of success really means.

- Your sense of yourself changes. Why even strive if you believe you are unworthy of any positive outcome or recognition as a result of your accomplishments?

- You're so frightened of failing or making a mistake that you won't even undertake the task.

- You mistrust your own talents and ability to complete a task because your self-confidence is shattered. There isn't much effort put into attempting a project.

- You feel inferior when you compare yourself to others, believing that no matter how much you achieve, it will never be enough.

- You begin to reason that even if you attain all of your objectives, you will still be unable to find true satisfaction and contentment in your life. So, what's the big deal?

Do any of these statements relate to you? Examine your fears to see if you fit into one of the categories above.

Conditioning of Fear

Fear is a natural survival tool that we all have. It functions as a means of safeguarding us against damage. However, the same fear that protects us can also be a hindrance in our lives.

Many of you may be held back by fear that is created by our culture, social structure, and ideals. Success in modern culture is measured in terms of income, fame, and prestige. We are graded based on how we compare to these standards. Fear takes over if your level of trust in your abilities isn't high enough to make you feel comparatively capable. Anxiety is a common result. This is the point at which the conditioning begins. This taught habit gets imprinted in the psyche as this fear is experienced over time.

You can find yourself highly intimidated by this type of fear conditioning. It makes you put off doing something important that can make a major difference in your life. The fear is reinforced even more each time it's put off and the training continues. You find yourself doing or acting in ways that are so unlike you because fear is a natural, physiological reaction.

Your self-image is ruined by fear training. It puts you under a lot of stress because you feel like you can't live up to your own personal standards, let alone the higher standards set by our culture.

Fear Is in Charge

Fear is a strong feeling. We can't cross a busy street without looking because we're afraid. Fear, on the other hand, prevents us from reaching our maximum potential. Fear is instilled in us as children because those who have power over us know that fear is an effective tool for control. This appears to work well when our parents warn us about the awful things that could happen if we:

- Run with a sucker in our mouth.
- Talk to strangers.
- Use alcohol, tobacco, or drugs.
- Fail to eat our veggies.
- Perform poorly in school.
- Break governmental and/or religious rules, etc.

It is the obligation of parents to educate their children about the perils of life. Education, on the other hand, educates while fear dominates. All too often, those in positions of authority choose fear above education. It's no surprise that fear-instilling strategies are frequently used by parents, teachers, coaches, political leaders, employers, and the media to achieve their goals.

Fear Has Its Origins

The dread of not surviving is our greatest fear. Another deep apprehension is that we won't be liked. When God or religion enters the picture, the two become inextricably linked. Some faiths claim that falling out of God's favor (being unloved) means spending an eternity in Hell (failure to survive).

Even without the influence of foundational religion, the dread of losing one's life or one's love is at the root of most of our fears. Choose any fear you're experiencing right now and trace it back to its source; I'm confident you'll discover that you're scared of personal harm (death at its most extreme) or emotional harm (the loss of affection from someone you care about).

Fear's Influence

Fear is nothing more than an emotion, although it's a powerful one. In childhood, fear helps us avoid unsafe situations. Healthy personal growth demands that we explore our worries now that we've reached maturity. Are our fears a help or a hindrance to us? So many of us go from one fear to the next every day without even recognizing it.

We lose our ability to be creative when we're afraid. Our bodies' resources are mobilized to deal with the feared occurrence when we are afraid, making it impossible to focus on anything else. If you've ever feared for the health and survival of a loved one, or feared an occurrence that would drastically affect your life, you've had this experience. When you're at the bedside of a sick loved one or experiencing a severe weather event, it's challenging to remain positive, creative, and active.

The worst of it isn't the temporary loss of inventiveness. Excessive concentration on a feared occurrence can actually invite that very event. The Law of Attraction states that we attract what we focus on. The vibrational frequency of the energy we make tends to attract occurrences with comparable vibrational frequencies.

We miss out on a lovely gift—the present—while we are fixated on a feared event. Because dreaded events are always in the future, we miss out on appreciating the current moment when we're focused on them. Unfortunately, one second at a time, we're missing out on life. The current moment is life. The only thing we have is the present moment. That is what life is all about. The past is no longer relevant; what matters now is what we've learned. The future is unpredictable; no one can forecast anything with any true precision.

Fear is similar to rocking on a chair; you expend a lot of energy but get nowhere. "Fear," as Yoda put it, "leads to anger; anger leads to hate; hate leads to pain."

LIVING IN FEAR

A fear-driven life is one in which fear is the primary motivator of one's thoughts, decisions, and actions. The majority of people live in terror. Our current culture encourages it. So, what does it mean to live a life motivated by fear?

Fear is the driving factor behind most thoughts and acts in a fear-driven life. Fear of death, loneliness, poverty, or pain are examples of such fears.

Fear stems from a lack of knowledge and faith in one's own divinity. A person is cut off from their divine essence, which is unconditional, limitless love, since they don't believe in their own divinity or that they're a co-creator of their own life. The level of terror represents the distance between an individual and their divinity.

This dread leads to a belief in one's own mortality, isolation, and scarcity in life, leading to the fear of death, loneliness, and poverty. The more afraid we are, the more we feel compelled to exert control over our lives by manipulating nature and everything else in order to prevent death, loneliness, poverty, and suffering.

Fear has the ability to immobilize us into inaction. It can make us lose touch with our emotions and thoughts, leading to incorrect decisions and judgments. It distorts our perceptions.

Any decision based on fear is likely to result in more dread and separation. It's contentious and self-centered rather than all-encompassing.

Understanding Fear

We are spiritual beings. We are love in its purest form—infinite, bright, and unconditional. Regrettably, we don't spend our lives as spiritual beings. In truth, we live as though we are nothing more than our bodies. As a result, we have limited awareness of and relationship with love.

Fear exists in the absence of love. We feel a sense of isolation from the oneness of all things when we are trapped in our egos. We feel lonely and insecure as a result of this separation, and thus scared. Fear arises as a result of our separation from our actual Essence.

The traits of a love-driven life are compared to those of a fear-driven life in the following ways:

1. Self-Determination

Love-Driven Life: The fear of death, pain, loneliness, and poverty is absent in the love-driven life. One doesn't feel compelled to manage or control life.

Fear-Driven Life: Despite accumulating wealth and power, there is no real freedom from the fear of death, agony, loneliness, and poverty.

2. The Present Situation

Love-Driven Life: One lives in the present moment.

Fear-Driven Life: One lives in the past and/or future.

3. Life Satisfaction

Love-Driven Life: There is inner calm, tranquility, and contentment.

Fear-Driven Life: There is no true serenity or peace of mind.

4. Observation

Love-Driven Life: One has a strong understanding of one's own strengths faults, and the fortitude to confront and address them.

Fear-Driven Life: Lack of understanding of one's own strengths and limitations, as well as a reluctance to turn inward to face one's true self. He is terrified.

5. Safety and Security

Love-Driven Life: One maintains the sense of having enough and trusts that providence will provide for them. Even when one has little, a sense of security remains.

Fear-Driven Life: Despite accumulating wealth and power, you always feel that there isn't enough. One feels uneasy.

6. Consequences

Love-Driven Life: A sense of stress-free fulfillment is always within reach.

Fear-Driven Life: Existence represents a perpetual struggle. Despite worldly triumphs, a sense of discontentment is standard.

Fear Has Many Faces

Fear can take numerous forms and can be focused either within or outwardly toward others. Anger and hatred, for example, are outward symptoms of fear directed at others, but guilt and shame are interior emotions of dread directed at ourselves.

In our daily lives, it might be difficult to perceive the many faces of dread. Most of them show themselves in very subtle ways, and if we aren't paying attention, we may miss them.

The majority of our fears are insidious, flying under the radar—creeping under our skin. It all starts with a single fearful thought, which leads to another and another and so on. Soon, it has taken on a life of its own before your eyes. This type of habit might literally cause terror in us if we're not vigilant or have inadequate self-awareness.

Fear is a common emotion, and we can feel it in ourselves virtually every day. When we aren't conscious of it, this inclination tends to repeat itself every time we let it emerge within us. The good news is that we can reverse this trend by practicing mindfulness and enhancing our self-awareness. The sooner we recognize this propensity in ourselves, the easier it will be to stop it or replace it with something more positive and healthier. We progressively loosen the grip that fear has on us if we do this on a regular basis.

Fear of Loss

All manifestations of fear can be linked back to the dread of loss. Here are a few things we don't want to lose:

- Personality (ego)
- Control
- Security
- Self-determination (free will)
- Good health (life)
- Abundance

The path to liberation is to transform fear-based behaviors, yet recognizing those patterns in oneself is difficult.

—Ingrid Bacci

We live in constant fear. The majority of everything we think, say, and do is motivated by fear. Our current civilization is centered on fear. We are afraid of losing our lives (death), our health (illness), our security (poverty), and our youth (aging). We are afraid because we fail to acknowledge that these changes are an inevitable part of life.

Our physical existence is finite. It is short-lived. Instead, we should accept and welcome this bodily reality with compassion. Fear can no longer exist in the presence of acceptance. It vanishes. Then, we can get down to the business of actually living and being in the moment.

Fear causes us to focus on the past or the future. We can more readily live in the present if we're not afraid. As a result, we must transform our fear-based culture into one based on "unconditional love." But how do we shift from a fear-driven lifestyle to one focused on "unconditional love"? We accomplish this by letting go of our ego. Our ego is the greatest impediment to leading a life based on "unconditional love."

The ego is defined as the part of consciousness that recognizes itself as distinct from others. As a result, the existence of ego entails a fundamental sense of separation from other living creatures. By removing our ego, we also remove our sense of separation from creation, God, or whatever name you want to give it.

(I use the word "God" with caution because it might signify different things to different people.) We all have our own preconceived notions of what God is. God refers to all of creation, nature, or our spiritual essence for our purposes.)

Fear and uncertainty arose from our estrangement from God. Thus, dread and insecurity, as well as a sense of isolation, are inextricably linked to the ego. The only way to get rid of all of these feelings of dread, uncertainty, and isolation is to get rid of the ego. When the ego is gone, we are left with only our genuine nature: unconditional love, radiance, wisdom, knowing, and being.

Fear in Everyday Life

Our daily lives provide several opportunities for spiritual growth. Every moment presents an opportunity to be more aware of what we think, say, and do. Every answer teaches self-awareness and the art of letting go.

Every step of the way, you'll be confronted with fear. Every sort of dread is present: small fear, large fear, actual fear, imagined fear. All fear is false, in reality, since fear is not our genuine essence. However, we are too ingrained in our fear-based culture to change with ease.

We attempt to alleviate our dread by acting, achieving, and looking externally—essentially, trying to keep our minds occupied and distracted from worry—and found momentary respite in the process. We, therefore, come to the incorrect conclusion that acting and achieving can help us overcome our fears. In truth, they just serve to divert our attention away from our anxiety. Our fear persists even after everything has been accomplished. However, doing and accomplishing has become a habit for us; a pattern of activity that we feel would enable us to overcome our fears.

Of course, we are mistaken, but like a drug addict, we find it impossible to break free from our addiction. We've been sucked in! Changing this behavior will take time and work, but I feel the end result will be worthwhile. It is, in fact, the only way to live a life free of fear.

Faith is believing something we can't see will happen; fear is believing something we can't see will happen.

The fact that our definitions of faith and fear are the same is very revealing. The only distinction is what you choose to concentrate on. It is trust if the focus is on what we want. Instead, if you choose to focus on what you don't want, it becomes a source of fear. This entails the following:

- Despair expects the unfavorable to occur,
- Hope expects the unfavorable to occur.
- As a result, we must be very selective about what we allow our minds to focus on.

Fear and Illness

Clinical experiments in medicine have revealed that persons who get sick often have personality features that appear to predispose them to disease. That explains why, despite the fact that everything else appears to be equal, some people develop diseases such as cancer while others do not.

It indicates that those who are continually worried and concerned are more prone to become ill. To put it another way, if you worry too much about having cancer, you can make yourself more likely to have it.

Doubts

Fear manifests itself in doubt. At the beginning of this spiritual activity, doubts are common. This is because in the beginning of our spiritual path, we don't have the "knowing," only the "believing," which is dependent on faith in others who have shown us the route. We must have faith that they are not deceiving us.

Only by practicing until believing becomes knowing - until we can taste the fruit for ourselves - will we be able to discover the truth.

Guilt, Anger, and Forgiveness

One who wishes to live a spiritual life must recognize, admit, and deal with his or her own wrath and guilt. When our ego is attacked, we become angry. When we examine it closely, we'll notice that rage is also a subliminal expression of fear. For example, we may become enraged at a careless driver that cuts into our route, putting our lives in peril. We were in danger of losing our lives or being physically harmed.

At first look, anger appears to be an emotion focused on something outside of ourselves, such as a person or an event that irritates us. However, a closer examination of our anger reveals that it is frequently directed toward ourselves as well. We can blame ourselves for not recognizing the dangerous motorist earlier and getting out of his way in the case of the reckless driver.

When we hold ourselves responsible for anything we did or didn't do that we believe is ethically wrong, we are said to be guilty. Anger and guilt are both suffocating feelings. They're not only detrimental to our spiritual growth, but they may even hinder us from progressing spiritually. They obstruct the flow of our genuine essence into our lives by creating blockages and resistance.

Negative emotions operate like cancer cells, spreading toxins throughout our entire well-being—physically, emotionally, cognitively, and spiritually—if not addressed. As a result, anger and guilt must be identified, acknowledged, and confronted, which can be accomplished through self-awareness and letting go. Forgiveness is one of the most powerful tools for letting go of our anger and guilt.

In reality, self-forgiveness is necessary for self-healing. We risk developing cancerous repercussions if we continue to harbor wrath and guilt within ourselves. We begin to heal on all levels—physically, emotionally, cognitively, and spiritually— the moment we decide to forgive ourselves and others who have given us these unpleasant emotions.

Fear Versus Love

To his grandson, an elderly man said, "I have two tigers imprisoned within me. One is known as love and compassion. The other is known as fear and fury."

"Which one will win, grandfather?" the young lad said.

"The one I feed," the old man said.

Our power is taken away by fear. When we live in fear and behave in fear, we are essentially giving up our authority. We're just reaffirming our view that we're not the spiritual beings we really are. We're telling ourselves that we need something outside of ourselves to make us feel better.

In our daily lives, we unfortunately, give away much too much of our power. We lose our power and move further away from our Essence of Love and wholeness whenever we make decisions based on fear rather than love. Every action, speech, and idea motivated by fear separates us from our spirituality.

To reclaim our power, we must act, speak, and think from a place of Love rather than fear. We require both guts and perseverance. We need to know that it is possible. Only then will we be able to establish true liberty. The only freedom you'll ever require is that of being free of fear.

The Cost of Fear

If we want to live a happy life, we must overcome our fears. The truth is that we pay a high price for our fear, both financially and spiritually. Fear is a costly habit all around. We spend a significant amount of money and effort attempting to overcome our fears.

The true cost, though, is to our spiritual development. We confirm our fear's "utility" and maintain its propensity in our lives every time we allow it to arise. Its power over us grows as its grasp on our life tightens. Fear and love cannot coexist, so as fear develops, so does love. They can't exist at the same time.

This is how we fall from grace—from a brilliant light being filled with unconditional love to a thick physical being filled with dread. We must now reverse this process, and to do so, we must be conscious of our thoughts in order to catch our fear and replace it with love as soon as we notice it.

Fear Can Be Experienced in Two Ways

Fear is the only thing we have to fear, so next, we'll look at why this is, what fear truly is, and how it can be turned into something powerful and productive for you with just a few easy methods that can be learned in under ten minutes.

This is crucial knowledge because, more often than not, fear inhibits us from making the necessary changes to enhance our lives. When change comes from the outside . . . a layoff, a death in the family, the loss of a relationship . . . fear paralyzes us. All of these events that bring about change cause people to be afraid. And how we deal with fear determines whether we have a positive outcome or none at all. A long time ago, an old buddy of mine put fear into perspective by linking each letter of the word F-E-A-R to another word, as follows:

F – FALSE
E – EVIDENCE
A – APPEARING
R – REAL.

FEAR is False Evidence Appearing Real.

Or another way of looking at it (which was my way for much of my life) . . .

F - FORGET
E - EVERYTHING
A - AND
R - RUN!!!

Fear is "an unpleasant, typically powerful emotion generated by anticipation or consciousness of danger," according to Webster's definition. "A pessimistic expectation about the future" or "a feeling that something is about to be lost or taken away" are two more ways to put it. Where does fear originate? Is it a result of the things that make us afraid? No. It originates from within ourselves. Fear is a feeling. Is a feeling a fact? When we experience fear, it certainly *feels* real. Is this, however, the case? No. Our emotions are the result of our imagination. Thoughts give rise to emotions.

It stands to reason that if we can produce the experience of dread, we should be able to manage it!

But how many times has your fear governed you? How many times has it made you sweat . . . almost stopped your breathing . . . made you feel strange in your stomach . . . kept you paralyzed?

Perhaps you've been laid off or are facing a layoff. Perhaps you're in the midst of a failing relationship or you're experiencing a financial crisis. Whatever the case may be. It's possible that's why you're reading this right now. If that's the case, I've got some wonderful news for you.

We experience terror at precise periods, which we refer to as "crises." This was noticed by the ancient Chinese, who also noticed that fear contains two components: worry and excitement.

They determined that a "crisis" indicates a conflict between danger and opportunity. Which one you use as a baseline for your situation is entirely up to you! And there's *more* good news. You have a choice.

As long as you're growing, fear will never go away. Taking constructive action is the only way to conquer fear. Walking directly through your fear is the only way to feel better about yourself.

Keep in mind that fear will always be present.

Fear is something that everyone goes through; therefore, you're not alone. Even if you've heard one or more of the five truths about fear just stated, here's a theory about fear that you might not have heard before. "Pushing through the dread is less terrible than living with the underlying fear that comes from a sense of helplessness," Susan Jeffers says.

That is extremely crucial. While it's difficult to comprehend while in the midst of the Dread, pushing through it is far less frightening than living with the fear.

Let's take a look at how this theory came to be. First and foremost, what do you do when you experience fear? It brings you to a halt. Your thought processes are disrupted, and all you want is for the terror to vanish. What do you normally do to get rid of fear? You either push it aside or tuck it inside and attempt to carry on as if nothing is wrong. And what happens as a result? Fear, anxiety, depression, and total paralysis follow.

That's a compelling justification for taking action—any action. The sooner you do it, the better. In fact, your sensory equipment swaps gears, and a true change occurs the minute you begin to act against the fear . . . all in a single moment. I've worked with thousands of folks just like you, and the response I've received has been overwhelmingly positive. It all adds up to an effective strategy for dealing with fear—removing it by facing it. "Fear isn't the problem," people often say after going through the process I'm about to detail.

It's how we deal with our fears. Fear can be viewed as a problem or an opportunity, to put it simply. We can experience it as either pain or excitement.

"I can't" is our response to fear when it manifests as pain or anxiety. When we feel it as excitement, on the other hand, we respond by saying, "I choose only to see the opportunity. I'm nervous about this," you might say, "but I'm going to do it anyway and see what happens!"

And this is crucial. When you're afraid, tell yourself that something is happening that deserves the emotion, but don't let it become a source of misery. Tell yourself there's a shift in the breeze. "Something has to change, and it's ME." And tell yourself that the fear will go away as soon as you change.

So, instead of fear, call it excitement, and be ready to deal with the situation right away, make the required changes, and raise your power grid up to a more comfortable level.

There's one more fear concept that we should consider. The egocentric belief that we can change what's going on around us causes the majority of our fear-based discomfort. Our fear, in reality, stems from a sense of helplessness, and our ego drives us to try to overcome external forces. It's an extremely vulnerable position.

The ego state tells us that power is "out there" and that our role is to exploit it to get what we want. What a difficult task! Not only do we have no idea what's out there, but we also have no control over it the majority of the time. It takes a lot of energy, the results aren't always predictable, and they don't always happen the way we want them to.

Self-love, on the other hand, allows you to declare that whatever strength you possess resides within you. Tell yourself, "It's always there for me when I need it, and I know how to use it. That's all I require. So let me put it to good use." This is a lot easier, and we have a lot more control over both the input and the outcome if we stick to this notion. As an antidote to fear, it makes sense to look at our fears from the inside out rather than the outside in. This is how we best work toward self-esteem and self-love.

"How does fear relate to change?" is the logical question here. The solution is straightforward. The majority of us are terrified of change. And we're driven by five fears.

Fear of the unknown is the first. We don't know what the change will bring; we're uneasy with what we have, but it's familiar, and giving up the familiar for the unfamiliar is difficult.

There's also the fear of failure. What if the change we bring about isn't beneficial? That is our egotistical fear regarding other people's opinions of us. What if we don't succeed? Aren't we going to be the laughingstock of our peers? So maybe it's best to stay the same!

The fear of commitment is the third fear that stands in the way of change. We know that if we keep our word, we'll do whatever we say we're going to do. But that entails some effort, and we'd rather not commit than jeopardize our reputation by breaking our word, especially to ourselves.

The dread of disapproval is the fourth fear on our list. Even if the adjustment we've made is better for us, other people may not like it. A friend gave me a simple example of this a couple of months ago. He made the decision to start an exercise routine and joined a gym. He worked out four days a week after his business day was finished. Was it good for him? Yes. But his wife, who was accustomed to having dinner at six o'clock, wasn't pleased, and she began to lecture him about it, telling him that all of his hard work was futile. She even modified meals to add more fat to her husband's diet on occasion, believe it or not. She was sabotaging his attempts because he was unsettling her sense of what was right, decent, and comfortable. I'd like to tell you that they were able to talk about it and come to an agreement, but that isn't the case. He was terrified of that conversation, so he stopped exercising in the evening and started exercising first thing in the morning. It wasn't a bad answer, but it avoided the problem, and he still fears her displeasure.

Finally, there is the terror of success. As much as we want to be the best, we're afraid that if we do, others will disapprove of us, shun us, think we're arrogant, and so on! As a result, we are limited by our fear of being above average!

Is it any surprise that most of us find it difficult to overcome our fears? Understanding what fear is and having the confidence to risk changing a situation might have truly life-changing consequences . . . for you!

My-mindguide.com

CONFRONTING YOUR FEARS

What's keeping you from achieving your goals and enjoying the life you want? When all the excuses are removed, the only thing left is fear—fear of doing whatever it takes to attain your goals.

Fear is one of our most fundamental impulses, and it's essential to our existence. It's tempting to dismiss dread as weakness, but this isn't the case. Cowardice is one of several possible responses to fear; courage is another. Fear isn't always a terrible thing. In actuality, it performs a useful purpose by safeguarding life and assisting us in avoiding danger.

Fear can cause our hearts to race and our adrenaline to rush. You surely know people who enjoy being terrified because they enjoy the sensation it gives them—thrill-seekers who seek out dangerous activities and exploit their fears to accomplish incredible feats. You don't have to enjoy fear to make it work for you, though, and you can apply the same principle to hobbies other than riding roller coasters, parachuting, or mountain climbing.

The goal is to recognize your worries and put them into context so that you can cope with them effectively. Before you react to your fear, take a moment to consider whether or not there is a genuine threat. If so, what exactly is the threat and what should you do to defend yourself? What's the source of the fear if there's no real danger?

What is it that you're frightened of?

What scares you the most? Flying? Do you want to jump out of a plane? Perhaps you have a fear of water. Dogs, cats, spiders, and snakes are examples of commonly feared animals. You may be apprehensive about crowds, public speaking, or even change. It's also possible that you're terrified of anything that concerns danger.

The truth is that life is a gamble. Any worthwhile endeavor will almost certainly entail some level of danger, whether physical, financial, or emotional. And it's only natural for those dangers to make people fearful. The ability to regulate and use the natural emotion of fear to one's benefit is what distinguishes achievers from non-achievers.

Fear that is out of control saps your self-esteem and ability to function. Fear that is well-managed and controlled can be incredibly beneficial because it can motivate you to assess dangers carefully and take efforts to limit and minimize them.

Fear-Based Responses
You can respond to fear in one of three ways:

1. Don't pay attention to it.
2. Stay away from it.
3. Face it head-on.

Ignoring fear—for example, thinking "I'm terrified to do something, but I'm going to do it anyway"—is the least efficient way to deal with it. You can't entirely dismiss your fear because if you don't address it, it will remain in your mind, producing tension and preventing you from performing at your best.

Denying fear—saying you're not frightened but simply don't want to do something—is a common way of ignoring the problem. If you know that performing a certain action will get you the results you want but you refuse to act, examine yourself carefully to see if you're actually rejecting a fear.

Fear-avoidance is only somewhat better than ignoring it. At the very least, when you avoid fear, you recognize it and are attempting to push it to the side and get around it. However, this is merely a band-aid solution to a long-term issue.

Confronting and overcoming your concerns is the most effective strategy in the short and long term. Recognize your fear, accept responsibility for it, deal with it, and strive toward your desired outcome. You eradicate the fear in the process.

When you confront your fear, you may shine a light on it, and you'll often discover that the dread isn't real. Consider when you were a kid and believed that monsters lurked beneath your bed or in your closet. When your parents entered the room and turned on the light, you could see that there were no monsters. It's not always easy to shine a light on grownup fears, but it's just as effective. Let's imagine you want to make an investment but are afraid of losing money. Put a spotlight on it. What are you truly terrified of? What are the worst-case scenarios? What can you do now to lessen the risk? Is your fear still legitimate if you do that?

Remember that there is freedom, achievement, and tranquility on the other side of any fear.

Overcome Your Fear and Overcome Your Fate

Is "fate" a part of your DNA? Is it a "habit pattern" that you unconsciously attract into your life? To realize your full potential, you must overcome your fears.

Perhaps we don't recognize it, but fear is always about something that will happen in the future. Even the terror one feels in the face of a present danger is a projection that the danger will materialize. While being aware of possible risks to one's physical well-being is beneficial, we must also acknowledge that fear prepares the body for instant action—flight or fight—which efficiently concentrates all of our physical and mental resources on the perceived threat.

This is all fine and dandy if you're dealing with a genuine threat. However, we are rarely confronted with serious dangers. The majority of the risks we see are ill-defined future events with a low likelihood of occurring. Despite this, we frequently experience fear, and fear is at the root of many of our actions. Is it healthy for us to be afraid, and why are we so afraid?

Overcoming fear is a simple one-step procedure: Put a stop to it! Fear is a limbic brain response to a perceived threat, whether genuine or imagined. It serves no purpose.

The only thing we have to fear is fear itself—an amorphous, irrational, and unjustified anxiety that paralyzes critical efforts to turn retreat into advance.

—Franklin D. Roosevelt

You can't get rid of fear, but you can develop a habit of saying "NO" to it and focusing on solutions and inspiration instead. If you repeat this process enough times, you'll unlock the door to your "destiny" and leave your old genetic "fate" behind.

Fear Not! You Can Overcome Your Fears!
You now understand the power that fear has over you. You may have blamed your inability to gain momentum on your lack of success mitigating fear. You must learn to overcome fear and let go of this albatross that prevents you from achieving your objectives. But how do you do it?

To begin, you must make the decision to change. You must decide whether to overcome your anxieties or let them derail your plans for the future. Yes, it's a choice that you must make. Spend some time alone to delve deep into the recesses of your heart and determine what concerns are preventing you from moving forward. Make a list of everything you can think of. You are the only one who completely understands the terror that holds you captive. You are the only one who has the ability to overcome your fear. Make the decision to let go of the victim role that fear has you playing, and put out the effort to remove it from your life. This is the first step in getting over your fear.

The next stage in overcoming fear is to become conscious of it. Recognize when fear has taken control of you and examine the situation. Recognize it and ask yourself, "What am I worried will happen to me?" What do I have to lose by giving it a shot? What am I truly terrified of? Make a list of your worries. Stop and consider how different your life would be if you were to overcome your fear. Consider how wonderful that would be. Consider the opportunities lost as a result of allowing fear to remain in control.

Try to face your worries now that you know what you're actually terrified of. If it's a lack of knowledge, look for ways to learn more about the issue. Take a class, conduct some online research, and find a mentor or a life coach. Make friends with those who will support and guide you. Dispel the fear by addressing all of the reasons for your dread. Your degree of confidence will rise as you gather more knowledge. Doubt and fear will be replaced by self-assurance.

Another method to boost confidence and reduce fear is to use positive self-talk. Repeating positive self-affirmations is a type of self-conditioning that eliminates subconscious misgivings. Remind yourself that you can accomplish anything.

Take action, first and foremost. Don't waste time hoping, thinking, or preparing. You certainly shouldn't wait for the perfect moment to act. Today is the ideal day to begin. Take a chance! Find out what you're good, at and do something about it right now. Being proactive is the best way to conquer fear. Your level of confidence grows with each effort.

Above all, have faith in your ability to overcome your worries and achieve your objectives. Believe in yourself and your ability to achieve great things in life.

Remember that having fears is a natural aspect of being human. It's a feeling similar to love, happiness, or melancholy. The issue occurs when fear has such a strong grip on your life that it prevents you from reaching your objectives. Fears are common among the most successful people. They simply don't allow their anxieties to hold them back. So, how serious are you about overcoming your fears? That's the million-dollar question.

Realize Your Full Potential

You won't be able to realize your full potential if you succumb to fear. You'll only be able to move forward with your life goals without the impediment of unnecessary dread after you address your fear, the source of your fear, and the chance of it occurring.

Do you need to face your fears?

Nope. Fear is a powerful motivator for many people. Fear inspires people and has done so for ages. Have you noticed the chaos? Death, battles, and devastation? Isn't it difficult to miss? If you've had you had your fill, there's good news. You have the ability to put an end to it.

Leaders take big risks, and the consequences are magnified in full view of the public.

Many people see the world through the lens of "fear." Leaders are making a big impact in the world. The road to success is paved with trial and error. Errors, on the other hand, are amplified and have far-reaching consequences. As a leader's worries grow, so does his or her terror. Fear obstructs reasoning and exacerbates the situation. Fear "makes itself real" in this way, and paranoia is soon justified.

How successful are you at putting out the fires you start or attract? Remember that fear, on the other hand, is not a conscious choice. It can be found in almost everyone. Many people are afraid of taking on leadership roles or pursuing fame and money. As such, fear is a bad predictor of success.

Insanity is defined as doing the same thing repeatedly and expecting different results.

—Einstein, Albert

Fear is attracted to itself (fear loss, and you lose; fear attack, and you invite violence.) You find what you're looking for, and your "experience" confirms your fears. It's tough to perceive the alternative once you've become engrossed in the drama.

Do you know why? Stopping fear and refusing to get drawn into the limbic brain's "fight or flight" reaction is the alternative. Staying mindful and finding answers is a decision. Then you'll need a strategy or vision for where you want to go, which you may train yourself to focus on instead.

It's a choice to allow inspiration to lead to solutions.

Everything you experience is a vibration, and a vibration, like a magnet, exerts a "pull." Energy draws other energy. Inspiration, combined with a laser-like focus on your vision or objective, leads to breakthroughs. That vision is appealing, and pursuing it is as well. That's outside the spectrum of "fear's" vibration. The higher the frequency of "expecting" things to work out, the more likely they are to go our way. That's how the Law of Attraction works.

The successful seek out and find solutions, often with stunning outcomes. Fear, on the other hand, is woven into the fabric of life. Many success stories reveal a never-ending battle with fear . . . wins and losses . . . struggle and gain. That's what happens when you don't fight fear but instead dance with it.

Where does all the fear come from?

Your forefathers and mothers. Fear of failure and "bonding" are two powerful genetic traits that stifle creativity and success. Everyone's ancestors lived under the control of a petty dictator at some point in their lives, whether as a wife, a slave, a servant, or a member of the military. All of our forefathers and mothers failed numerous times, often enduring great pain and suffering. Your fear is a component of your genetic makeup. And for this reason, you have the ability to alter it.

You're not getting the results you want?

The only thing standing between you and what you want is fear. Your own genetic patterns are the only thing holding you back, aside from an old habit. This is referred to as "fate" by some. You've learned your lesson.

Your existence is a mirror of your genetic code—or your fate. Your experiences were built on that subconscious pattern. You've changed and expanded it over the years. You have the power to influence your destiny. Is it time to make another change?

If you're not having the success you want, it's time to expand your horizons. After all, Your fear of change and loss can also shift.

Living with fear is living in chaos.

If you don't overcome your fear, you'll keep fighting yourself, living in anxiety and tension, and eventually, the fear will win out, and you'll get what you fear, along with whatever success you can hold on to. It's time to let go of that tension. Life can be simple, enjoyable, and successful. All you have to do now is choose it, act on it, and live your vision. You're waking up if you're upset because it seems too simple to be true.

The natural creative process is one of contraction and growth.

You've outgrown your old thought patterns (and worries), and that's the only thing holding you back. How did you figure that out? You're itching for more. You feel constrained and blocked, and nothing you try seems to work. You feel "contracted, boxed in, and constrained" in comparison to where you wish to be.

When you have the feeling that you aren't obtaining what you want and don't know how to achieve it, that feeling is keeping you locked in your current situation. The confrontation between vibrating or signaling what you want and your fear is referred to as *conflict*. *Stress* is the term for those contradictory emotions.

Get out of there as soon as possible. Simply recognize that your unconscious worries are the only thing limiting you. When you allow fear to run rampant in your imagination, you are inviting the "destiny" you fear.

Get yourself away from whatever isn't working.

You can't push through a genetic fear—and that's what's limiting your advancement—so give up hard work until you can broaden your self-image. You desire what you want, but you're afraid of what will happen to you if you receive it (unconsciously). Overcoming your fears can help you break your undesirable habit.

As long as he doesn't comprehend his distinctive teleology, which has all the inevitability of fate, every individual behaves and suffers in line with it.

—Adler, Alfred

How do you know if you're being held back by fear?

Is fear a part of your daily routine? Do you have apprehensions about going out into the world or increasing the scale of your business? Are you looking for an altogether new way to live? Being more . . .growing . . . claiming new experiences . . . taking a chance . . . fresh learning . . . giving up what you thought you wanted . . .

Is it unsettling to change your daily routines, behaviors, and habits? It should be. You've progressed and expanded, but you can't seem to figure out how to reach where you want to go.

Your fear is interfering with your inspiration and clouding your vision.

When you see fear as "the habit" that attracts the precise thing you fear, you may overcome it. So, Pay attention to what you're saying to yourself. Fear might also take the form of avoidance (e.g., "I don't care about money; if the Universe wanted me to be rich, I would be).

Over the millennia, throughout the course of many deaths and tremendous anguish and suffering, the fear of "breaking free" has developed. Yet, by understanding it for what it is and talking yourself into your "now," when you are safe and your concerns are no longer valid, you can overcome it.

Nothing can be removed, but it can be transformed into something else. It will be yours if you can build a bridge from fear to success in a major way. When you've overcome your fear, you'll need a "bridge of thoughts" to help you get to your vision (target). To move your feelings and point of attraction from fear to solutions, you'll need a "destination."

What evidence do you have that it's working? You begin to feel optimistic and anticipate the new success you desire. From doubt to expectation, your feelings (and point of attraction) alter.

What you expect is always what you get. There are no exceptions. Use that data to pinpoint your location, and you'll be able to feel exactly what you want.

Once the barrier has been removed or softened, your inspiration will lead you to new options. Compare the new possibilities to your vision and take action if they match; if not, wait for choices that feel good and do match your vision.

Make it simple and enjoyable.

Spend time in nature and ask questions to cleanse your thoughts, open your heart, mind, and body. Look for answers and follow your intuition. You've got this.

When you start to see fear as genuine and allow it to control your life, it becomes dysfunctional. You begin to create a web of fear-based reality around yourself over time. The web becomes stickier, the more you give in to dread, and it prevents you from achieving your true desires. If you give in to fear repeatedly, you'll get stuck and find you're unable to go forward or distinguish between dread and reality.

Fear is constantly used by the ego against you. It can obscure your thoughts by filling your mind with restrictive beliefs that repeat themselves like broken records. Fear spreads beyond your thoughts, sending messages to your brain and presenting itself as a web of bodily tension, pain, and illness. Fear slowly eats away at your nervous system, robbing you of your capacity to relax and feel secure.

Your ego has the ability to outsmart you strategically. When you take a risk, how does your ego know to turn up the terror volume? Pursuing your aspirations or greatest desire is dangerous indeed. Fear detects that you're not simply venturing beyond the known but also pursuing your true desires. As a result, you'll be twice as vulnerable. Your ego comes to your aid, resisting your efforts and attempting to return you to a secure and familiar place. This dynamic gets people so engrossed in their daily lives that they may forget or abandon their goals. Fear, in the end, is a toxin that pollutes your mind, body, and spirit. Fear stifles your ability to express yourself, causing physical harm. So, here you are, facing the huge wave of life, which is beckoning you to jump in and live a life free of fear. You may either ride the wave and "go with the flow," or you can cling to the past and reject life. (Hint: jumping in is a lot more satisfying!)

Before you jump into life, there are three things you should know:

1. Don't Fight Your Fear – "What one resists persists," and fear is a perfect example of this. Fear is a natural response to growth and change. Fear alerts our brain to protect us from "actual" damage when the conditions are perfect. Fear will retaliate with a vengeance if you oppose or push it away.

2. Don't Be Afraid to Act – Fear will feed itself if you react to it in any manner, creating an even stickier web. If you ignore or bury your fear, it will resurface at some point, most likely when it's most inconvenient for you.

3. Don't Pass Judgment on Fear – Fear is dedicated to keeping you safe. Fear will feel more menacing if you evaluate it as wrong, pulling out all the stops to hold you back and keep you safe.

To build a life free of fear, follow these five steps:

1. Pay Attention to Your Fear – Recognize that fear isn't real, no matter how real it appears to be. To help you see where you stop and your fear begins, go within or seek advice from someone you trust. Fear can be observed by listening for its voice. Fear can take the form of your own or an authority figure's voice. Begin to recognize fear for what it is: a broken record. Recognize that it is truly attempting to keep you safe. Space will open up as you learn to view and experience fear as something separate from yourself, allowing you to breathe better and see things more clearly.

2. Be Afraid – Fear is frequently linked to physical or emotional pain in the past. Fear saves us from "getting there" rather than feeling and digesting the suffering. Feeling your fear is a step forward! The web's hold on you weakens the more you say yes to dread and welcome it. When you strip away the layers of dread to reveal plain fear, not only does it loosen its grip on you, but it also reduces the drama in your life. "What if I lose my job?" is an example of peeling back fear by pursuing a chain of fear-based thoughts. "What if I lose my money?" you might wonder. "What if I lose *everything*?" Allow your mind to continue the chain of thoughts until it reaches the point where fear is the only thing remaining. Acknowledge your fear. Feel the fear and the emotions that come with it, noting where the fear is

located in your body. Then, when you exhale, take a deep breath and let go of the dread. Try to keep feeling and letting go of dread without succumbing to the web of convoluted ideas and drama.

3. Love Your Detachment – A space will open up when you learn to see fear as separate from yourself and feel it for what it is. Before moving on, it's critical to first fill this place with love. Only by detaching from fear with love can one fully live beyond it. This entails realizing that you are not your fears and embracing the part of yourself that gave rise to the anxiety. Childhood, a recent disappointment, a self-saboteur or victim mentality, low self-esteem, or insecurity are all possibilities. It's more vital to embrace who you have been in the past, who you are now, and who you will become with love, compassion, and kindness than it is to identify the root of your prior hurt. Love is the most powerful tool for dissolving the tangled and sticky web of fear.

4. Express Yourself – With a fresh foundation of love, you may begin to move and express yourself without fear. You'll rip away any vestiges of a physical web that may have attached itself to your body when you move and express yourself. Stretching, yoga, dance, free movement, exercise, and deep conscious breathing will continue to loosen the web's grip and create fresh space for living without fear. Allow yourself to move from a place of love and expression (not an attempt to rid yourself of fear). Feel your breath go throughout your body as it cleanses, clears, and opens the regions that are closed, painful, tight, or blocked as you breathe. Get out of the house or office, mix, network, discuss ideas, do

something creative, or take a chance to express yourself. Get your blood pumping!

5. Commit and Expand – You'll feel yourself expanding and your energy growing as you move and express yourself. You'll start to attract new individuals and new experiences as a result of your efforts. Choose a mission or a commitment to guide this fresh burst of energy. "What do I want my life to be about when I get out of bed in the morning?" ask yourself. "What is it that I genuinely want to accomplish?" "Do I have a cause or a project that I'm passionate about?" You'll have something greater and more tempting than dread awaiting you every day if you broaden yourself and choose what you're devoted to. Stay dedicated and keep taking action, knowing that you're now weaving a new web of expression, joy, and fulfillment.

Living without fear necessitates dedication. Once you've mastered it, you'll experience a tremendous sense of freedom, ease, and fulfillment, as well as a life beyond your wildest dreams.

Common Fears

We want to think of ourselves as special and unique, yet when it comes to fear, we are rarely alone. Fear of failure and its partners, fear of success, fear of scorn, fear of discomfort, and even fear of the spotlight are all fears that prevent most of us from achieving our goals. Let's take a look at each one separately.

It's perfectly understandable to be afraid of failing. Nobody enjoys failing. We don't want to let anyone down, including ourselves. However, just because you make a mistake or aren't successful right away doesn't imply you've failed. Trial and error is the most common method for resolving problems in life. You haven't failed if you make a mistake; you've simply learned a strategy that didn't work. None of the amazing technologies that we now take for granted were created on the first attempt. Even the best athletes don't always succeed. Consider the following scenario to help you understand your fear of failure: Some of the things you try won't work, but that just means that the things you tried didn't work. You didn't fail, and you're not a failure, as long as you try again.

Consider the fear of success, which is the polar opposite of the fear of failure. The fear of success can be almost as paralyzing as the fear of failure, and it frequently *follows* the fear of failure. Some people let their fear of success sabotage their efforts because they're worried about what will happen if they succeed. Success can be both exhilarating and terrifying. With a plan to manage your success, you can overcome your fear of success.

Another prevalent phobia is that of being mocked. We don't want to be mocked. You have no control over what other people think or say, but you do have power over how you respond. Of course, ignoring scorn is much easier said than done—particularly when it comes from someone we care about. It's helpful to try to figure out what motivates the person who is ridiculing others; most people who ridicule others are striving to hide their own flaws and insecurities. Consider utilizing semi-agreement to defuse the ridicule: "Sure, I'm insane for attempting this, but at least I'm trying—and you never know; I could succeed." You won't have to say anything if you succeed.

The fear of being uncomfortable has a lot of power. Most of us like to stay in our comfort zones, surrounded by people and things we are acquainted with. It's certainly easier to do what's convenient, such as watching TV instead of going to the gym or staying in a dead-end job instead of doing what it takes to get out of it. But doing what feels good today will almost certainly lead to something even worse tomorrow. Staying comfortable means remaining stuck in a rut and not attempting to improve.

It's also understandable if you're afraid of being in the spotlight. Every day, we witness the most personal parts of politicians' and celebrities' lives being scrutinized by strangers, and while scandals and gossip excite us, *we* don't want to be the subject of such scrutiny. Fortunately, most of us do not have to be concerned about this. However, even if your "fame" is minor, such as giving a presentation in front of a group or getting recognized for an accomplishment, you may be afraid of being the center of attention. That said, you can conquer your fear of being in the spotlight with practice and preparedness.

Make use of visuals as a powerful tool. It will almost certainly happen if you concentrate on your fear and visualize the worst-case scenario. Instead, picture your success and the outcomes you desire; then visualize yourself doing the measures necessary to achieve them. When it's time to do whatever it is that makes you nervous, you'll be calm and confident since you've already done it in your mind and know it'll work.

It's also crucial to understand that fear is contagious. Other people's concerns have the potential to infect you. These people are sometimes terrified because they truly want to protect you; other times, they display fear in the hopes of stopping you because they're worried that your success would expose their own flaws. In either situation, you must inoculate yourself against other people's worries by using a mental vaccine.

Unfortunately, conquering fear isn't something that most of us can do once and never have to deal with again. Fear is a common emotion that you will encounter on a regular basis. The trick is to not let your anxieties paralyze you into inaction, but rather to channel them into preparation for achieving your objectives.

On The Other Side of Fear Lies Freedom
The majority of the time, what we seek is on the other side of fear, but many people are paralyzed by the dread of the unknown in their pursuit of desires. When we decide to confront our worries, we discover that liberation awaits us. Despite the potential rewards, many people are nevertheless hesitant to take a risk.

Why? Is it worth the risk of trying to live your aspirations and failing? Do you believe you lack confidence in your abilities? Are you afraid of losing everything if you venture into the unknown?

Well, there is always a danger in anything; that is life. However, you'll never know if you never try. And if you have dreams, they indicate that you want more from life—and that your desires are on the other side of fear.

First and foremost, you must be dedicated to the path of discovering what lies beyond your anxieties. True, there isn't a map for it, but do you have one for your current existence? So it's about having the courage to take a leap of faith and move towards your ambitions, despite the fear, doubts, or grief you may face.

Many people out there are currently going through difficult times. When the blows are coming at you hard, it's difficult to maintain your beliefs. And you know how it feels when you're simply trying to keep your head above water.

On the other hand, what's on the other side of fear is merely a hazy awareness of what's holding you back and why you're not reaching your full potential. And while it's easy to see yourself as the joyful, kind, and successful person you want to be, you must also do the walk. You understand, however, that hoping, thinking, and wanting isn't the same as doing and becoming.

Fear Isn't Your Worst Enemy

You're the worst adversary you've ever had! The reason is straightforward. You refuse to take control of your situation, yet you whine about wanting more, about a lack of abundance, or about your whole existence. However, you'll be astounded to learn that you're the only one who controls your own future. You, and only you, are a celestial being!

While you're sitting on your couch, God or whatever divine being you believe in isn't going to bring you over the fear barrier to the things you want. Things won't happen unless you take action. Recognize that fear is a normal aspect of life. Many of your concerns have their origins in your childhood and how you were raised. However, you frequently bury your anxieties and avoid confronting them.

Furthermore, you disregard the source of your anxieties to the point that they come back to bother you as an adult. We've all experienced fear at some point in our lives. It could be a fear of letting go, losing control, or simply pretending to be someone you're not.

To get past fear, you may need to overcome crippling worries that hinder you from moving forward in life. You must accept the fact that you'll never have everything figured out. You have a long journey ahead of you—and there's always a new terminus upon arrival.

Face Your Fears

So, it's time to wake up and take control of your emotions. It makes no difference whether you have to push through your worries to find out what's on the other side. You must move forward. I can state that many of the circumstances in my life have pushed me to the edge of terror for many years. You accomplish it in tiny or huge ways.

You can't blame your dissatisfaction or lack of achievement on circumstances or events. That is a simple solution. Are you deceiving yourself to make yourself feel better? Do you persuade yourself it's not your fault but that "life" is the problem? Get serious; there is only one reason you lie to yourself, and that reason is fear—the fear of telling, possessing, or accepting the truth. You're afraid of having to be honest with yourself. The real reason is that instead of pointing your finger, you might have to look in the mirror. Fear and doubt are the two most powerful destroyers of dreams. Whatever the situation may be, everything you desire lies on the other side of fear. The righteous challenge involves letting go and facing your fears.

The list of uncertainties goes on and on, affecting every part of your existence. It could be personal, emotional, professional, physical, or mental in nature. You may be afraid of being alone, but you also fear falling in love. Furthermore, you may be terrified of both failing and of succeeding.

My-mindguide.com

ON THE OTHER SIDE OF FEAR IS FREEDOM

Change, of course, can be frightening. You can't predict what will happen if you take a chance and step into the unknown. Uncertainty can be enticing and frightening, making you question yourself, your decisions, and your goals. However, being open to the out-of-the-box experience of what lies on the other side of uncertainty is an important element of the life journey.

Just keep in mind that everything in our world has an equal balance. When doubt strikes, you must have faith in your ability to overcome it. You gain the strength to tolerate suffering when it strikes. When fear strikes, you receive love to help you overcome it. All you have to do now is keep going. You can always find a way to the other side of whatever life throws your way.

"At the end of the day, we all know that the other side of any fear is freedom."

You must progressively alter your mindset and approach as it relates to difficulties and events. By that, I mean that you must take control of your life and never rely on others to make you happy. And you must concentrate on yourself because liberation is on the other side of what you fear and in the most unexpected places. Everything else will fall into place if you believe that freedom is a choice.

Allow Your Fear to Strengthen You

There's no denying that life can be harsh at times. However, if this proves the case, choose to be stronger. You're not a machine, so take a break when you need to. Make the effort to figure out what's going on. However, don't be broken by uncertainty, grief, or anguish. And don't let doubts keep you from achieving your goals.

In any case, don't let fear steer you in the wrong direction. Allow it to strengthen you by keeping you focused on your goals and ambitions. You must step out of your comfort zone, set your sails, trust in the direction you are taking, muster the bravery to leave the beach, and trim your sails as you go. I'm confident in your ability to complete this task.

Remind yourself that on the other side of fear is whatever you want in life. It's all within your grasp, whatever it is. Face your anxieties head-on and allow them to strengthen you. As soon as you recognize your worries, you can put an end to their ability to rule your life, allowing you to live your best life yet.

Taking the Road Less Traveled on the Other Side of Fear

Following your heart, pursuing your aspirations, and traveling on the other side of fear won't always be simple—especially when other things are going on in your life. It's difficult to keep going when the waves appear to be approaching.

However, you must realize that the mountains you're confronting are primarily mental. When you start climbing, you might be startled to discover that they aren't as huge as you anticipated. There's no such thing as an insurmountable difficulty in life.

Understanding this will prevent you from getting lost in whatever is raging around you. A storm can't last forever, so know that once you cross the threshold of dread, all will be well.

There is some anxiety and awkwardness when you first leave the coast, but you learn to deal with it. So, the next time you have a choice between something you are afraid of and something that's inside your comfort zone, I hope you select the other side of fear because it contains a greater value than anything you will ever know.

Fear is a Decision

It isn't difficult to broaden one's vision to see that the basic geopolitical battle is one of fear vs. love. On a grand scale, we are witnessing a screenplay that each of us in the human condition has agreed to by being born into a situation of separation, struggle, and survival.

Going beyond simply political or psychological perspectives has the advantage of allowing us to see the clash of ideals (fear vs. love) as essential to our common dilemma. Attempting to tackle the world's issues from the same mental state that generates them is futile and, in fact, exacerbates the situation.

This is why it's so critical to comprehend fear right *now*. We will choose to remain in a state of emotional reactivity to events rather than an intelligent response if we don't comprehend fear. This is precisely what the "powers that be" are banking on to keep their dream and addiction to power and control alive.

So, what exactly is fear? Nothing more than a collection of thoughts or beliefs linked to specific bodily responses to stress or trauma. Chronic fear states are a mental construct that is entwined in deeply held, unconscious beliefs in the form of mental imagery. As previously stated, these beliefs can stem from survival instincts, but once supported and reinforced by deliberate media and constantly reinforced low-level cultural values, they can become so indelibly imprinted in the mind that many people build an identity based on the assumption of fear as natural, justified, and even virtuous.

To put fear in its proper place and return it to its original purpose as a simple biological reflex, we must first understand fear's flaws as a psychological emotion. What is the purpose of fear? Consciousness constriction, dependence on conditioned beliefs, and exacerbation of the conditions that encourage dread. Fear, like a mind virus, has the potential to destroy the host in its all-consuming quest to infect everything it comes across. Fear is self-defeating and life-denying in the end.

In fact, the basic tension between love and fear is a dualistic issue. Duality is a state of awareness in which opposites are perceived as real. We've divided our minds to see "this" and "that" as essentially different things. We are ascribing the idea of separation as genuine by separating our perceptions in this way. And in doing so, we unintentionally reaffirm the unconscious dread that we are also isolated . . . from nature, each other, and even whatever created us. As a result, the concept of separation and duality is fundamentally frightening, touching a deep unconscious nerve in our minds that tells us we are essentially weak, helpless, and condemned to die after living a worthless existence for no reason other than to suffer. This is classic ego propaganda, designed to keep you down, with the ego being comprised of separate beliefs and the dread they encourage.

The state of our world as we see it through the lens of duality serves as an intricate mirror for each of us to see where we are in our growth and where we are at the crossroads. We're being forced to evolve to the next developmental stage of the species, when we transcend the "shell" of the individuated ego and its fears to become a unified organism expressing both the individuality of its components and that which unites us all— our common essence or spirit, if you will.

As a result, fear might be viewed as a limited condition that only serves as a catalyst for moving beyond it. Fear is always contractive, whereas love is always expansive and inclusive. Can't we simply change our views about the meaning of these apparent opposites and bring the whole issue to a close if the duality of love and fear is only a part of our brains' condition at an early stage of development? Which of the two emotions, love or fear, do you prefer? This could be one of the most crucial questions you ever ask. Which of the two do you think provides the most grounded perspective? Consider the fact that only one of these polar opposites can be true in the end. Where does this lead you if only dread is real? What happens to fear if only love is real?

Given that fear is constrictive and love is expansive, which do you believe must "win" in the end? Do you perceive fear reaching out to grasp and suffocate love? This is incompatible with fear's hostility to that which unites rather than divides. Fear, alas, can only lead to destruction. Separation digs a hole only to discover more separation; a seemingly endless pit of futility. Love, on the other hand, looks at fear and thinks to itself, *This, too, may be loved into wholeness.*

Let's describe fear as a space where we haven't yet allowed love to infiltrate. Fear is like an empty room with no windows or light to provide context. When we open the door to the notion that fear doesn't exist beyond our imagination, love is the light that floods the room.

We're all extremely powerful beings. YOU ARE AN EXTREMELY POWERFUL PERSON. We've all have been given the ability to make choices. And now, hopefully, you understand that fear is a choice, not a "given," and that you have the power to say "no more" to fear and instead choose love. My personal assurance is that unlike the remorse and shame we frequently feel when we succumb to fear, you will never regret that decision. Fear has a tendency of wreaking havoc on our bodies, thoughts, and relationships. Now is the time to decide "I'll do my best to recognize when fear has taken over my thinking, and I'll do everything I can to use the power I've been given to choose love. And if I do succumb to fear, I'll forgive myself and realize that I'll always have another opportunity to choose love."

SIMPLE QUESTIONS YOU NEED TO ASK YOURSELF WHEN YOU BECOME FEARFUL

One of the greatest discoveries a man makes, one of his great surprises, is to find he can do what he was afraid he couldn't do.
—Henry Ford

There isn't a single person who hasn't felt terrified or faced unpleasant conditions that have made them anxious. Fear is an emotion that most of us despise but that we will all deal with at some point in our lives.

What is it that you're frightened of? When you think about it, what makes your heart stop? What is the one thing that stresses you out the most? What is it that you're most concerned about?

Are you, like so many of us, concerned about your future? Do you have concerns about your job security or the future of your children? There are plenty of things to make us fearful. Life is unpredictable, and we develop a fear of the future as a result of the uncertainty and unknown.

If you're like the majority of us, you'll need to cultivate the correct mindset in order to overcome your worries. It's never a good idea to live in dread. You need to confront your anxieties and devise strategies to prevent having to deal with them repeatedly.

Find the source of your anxiety and confront it. The beautiful thing about facing your concerns is that once you've dealt with them, they won't bother you anymore. You'll also get stronger and more capable of dealing with other unpredictable events in your life.

When you're afraid, ask yourself these questions to help you handle your fears.

1. Is it true that I'm afraid for the appropriate reasons?
Fear is beneficial because it keeps us protected. Make the most of your fear by putting it to good use. Don't spend your life being afraid. Make your fear a motivator to pursue your dream. Don't let your anxieties about the future overtake you; instead, channel them toward improving your future. Face your concerns by directing them to areas that will help you achieve your goals.

2. Do my anxieties make me feel good or bad?
What are the things you're most afraid of? Are they favorable or unfavorable? Which fears do you find yourself focusing on the most? Rather than being afraid of situations over which you have no control, focus your energies on making your life easier and less stressful. Take the time to focus on the positive rather than the negative. Fear is the only thing we have to be afraid of. Roosevelt, Franklyn

3. What significance do I place on challenges?

Consider this: what are you concentrating on? Are you giving your anxieties a life by thinking about them all the time? If that's the case, fight the impulse to worry and recover your power by focusing on what you want to do. Concentrate on the things that will help you grow as a person.

4. Am I allowing fear to take over my life?

You will never enjoy your life if you live it in fear. There is always something to be afraid about. Why waste time worrying about things that may or may not occur and over which you have no control? Fear robs you of your joy, so if you want to be happy, you must get rid of it. You can't appreciate life if you're terrified.

5. Do I have real or imagined fears?

You often cultivate fear when there is nothing to be afraid of. Do you give a circumstance more power than it deserves when it arises? Don't give your fear the ability to grow. Remember that things always appear to be worse than they are.

6. What can I take away from my fears?

Discover the lessons that life is attempting to teach you. Don't lose out on the chance to receive the message you've been sent. Find out what terrifies you the most and what you can do to minimize your fear whenever you're afraid.

Our anxieties will never go away, but you must learn to manage them rather than allow them to control you. Live your life with confidence, expecting the best, and those dreams of yours will come true. If you're afraid, figure out why you're afraid and find a solution; if you can't stop worrying about it, accept that there's nothing you can do about it.

Ego-Centered vs. Task-Oriented

According to recent studies, task-oriented people stick with tasks longer, prefer more difficult tasks, work harder, and perform better under pressure.

Our perspectives can shift from one moment to the next, and it takes time to develop mental habits that ensure our thoughts don't fail us when we need them most.

Three Developmental Stages (Ericsson)

1. Quick Grows – The focus is on learning and progress rather than winning or outcomes.
2. Growth Slows – One's emphasis changes to winning/losing, which we have no control over, causing anxiety.
3. Growth Halts – We give up due to frustration and perceived failure.

Setting Objectives

We must always be striving toward a defined goal; otherwise, we'll find ourselves swimming in circles and fighting with ourselves, which will lead to self-defeating actions. If we allow our mental resources to be directed in ways that aren't in our best interest, it's all too easy to get depressed.

Only by engaging in self-defeating behavior will we be unable to achieve goals that are within our direct control.

Set goals that are within your power but just a bit out of reach. When we set the right goals, fear loses its place in our mental processes.

Setting objectives that are just outside of our reach—thus generating effort in the pursuit of the aim—is critical to motivating ourselves in a way that ensures action.

It is beneficial to write down daily goals, as it:
1. Makes productive use of your energy.
2. Binds you to a mission.
3. Proves a good reminder of what you're doing.

Confidence
- Conceit – "I'm great; you stink."
- Arrogance – "I'm great, and I'm telling everyone about it."
- Self-assurance – "I'm OK."
- Passive – "I'm not very good."
- Pessimism – "You're great, but I'm a jerk."

Conceit and both pessimism include comparing yourself to others, making your mental state dependent on their performance.

The finest way to excellent performance is confidence – it's a competition with oneself, a war of self-mastery. The most consistent characteristic distinguishing highly successful athletes from less successful athletes is confidence.

There are four ways to build confidence:

1. Previous Performance Achievements – We acquire confidence by learning and reinforcing what we have done well in the past.

2. Vicarious Experiences – If someone else can do it, we can do it too.

3. Verbal Persuasion – What we most frequently express to ourselves programs the brain's neuro-pathways. Consistently assuring ourselves that we can accomplish something boosts our confidence.

4. Physiological States – Being able to regulate our bodies and have them perform the way we want them to boosts our self-assurance.

Anxiety

Anxiety serves as a natural "alarm system" for us. We don't want to be anxiety-free, but we do need to learn to manage it. When our bodies activate our alarm system when there is no threat, our minds don't work at their optimum level.

How Can We Manage Our Anxiety?

Setting proper objectives that inspire us in the right way, reducing worry, is the most essential technique to lessen and ultimately control anxiety.

Anxiety and guilt make our minds wander all over the place.

Thoughts quickly become mental representations in the mind, and asking ourselves not to do something can feel like programming ourselves to do it.

Putting out more mental effort rather than focusing on our flaws, we should focus on the positive aspects of what we accomplish.

Making a Decision

Making appropriate decisions on a regular basis is essential for high performance. Even if we have all of the skills and knowledge in the world, we'll be useless if we don't make good decisions.

Fear is usually "managed" in one of three ways.

1. Allow yourself to be swayed by it. (This strategy embeds fear—and exacerbates it.)

2. Pretend it isn't there. (This causes internal strife, exacerbating the consequences.)

3. Examine what fear is trying to tell you. (This gives you the opportunity to appreciate your warning system for keeping you safe while also telling yourself that you've got this!)

You may squeal, jump, run, or say something wrong before you have a chance to consider how best to proceed. After all, fear demands an immediate response. Don't be embarrassed by it. Regain your composure and reflect on what you've just learned. As you become more resourceful and fearless, it requires work to be able to use curiosity and listen to your body and mind.

Consider the following questions:

- Does the fear make me aware of a real and urgent threat to my health?
- Is my worry a warning sign that something bad is about to happen?
- Is the fear a "remembered" story from the past that no longer serves me?
- Is the fear pointing to an area of my comfort zone where I want to expand?

You will feel more in control if you acknowledge the sensations you feel in your body and learn to recognize what fear is trying to tell you.

When our fears are triggered by interactions with other people, we can usually trace them back to how we expect them to react and respond (e.g., get angry, hate us, reject us, hit us, fire us).

That's when you need to pay attention to your concerns and put in place the proper precautions to take the risk, such as:

- Take a deep breath, relax your posture, and settle down. (Your behaviors will be unconsciously mirrored by the other person.)

- Figure out what about the circumstance scares you the most. (This determines if the threat is real or imagined.)

- Consider how they might feel if they were in danger. (Do they feel challenged, insufficient, or unloved?)

- Visualize a favorable outcome from the situation. (This causes a mental shift.)

- Find a win-win situation for both you and the other person. (After all, you don't want to win the fight but lose the war.)

- Decide on your goals. (I aim to keep this relationship going.) I plan to speak with boldness. I intend to listen attentively and lovingly.)

- Use effective communication skills to express how essential this relationship is to you, as well as how you are feeling right now.

- Pay attention to how they are feeling in return, without passing judgment or internalizing your kneejerk reaction. (It's about them and how they feel, not you.)

Observe how you're breathing and feeling, as well as how your thoughts are moving, at each stage of this process. Are you inhaling and exhaling more deeply? Are you more at ease now? Do you have a more positive outlook?

Fear defeats more people than any other one thing in the world.
—Ralph Waldo Emerson

Have you recently been afraid? Were you apprehensive about trying something new? To step outside of your comfort zone? You didn't want to say anything because you were afraid it would cause a fight? Did you confront it head-on or did you back away and flee? What did your reaction make you feel like? Is it better to be powerful or powerless?

"An unpleasant emotion generated by the notion that someone or something is dangerous, likely to cause pain, or a threat." That's the general definition of fear provided by any given dictionary. From this point forward, however, I urge you to re-define fear as follows: "This sense of fear is alerting me to an opportunity to become more completely aware of my surroundings and connect with my inner power to deal with whatever is happening."

We can mature and embrace each unpleasant sensation as an opportunity for growing and enriching our life experience, just as children first love sweets and then develop a taste for the full palette of flavors as they mature to adulthood—bitter coffee and endive, spicy chili peppers, salty anchovies, and sour lemon. Here are some strategies to create a fearless mentality to help you reframe your sentiments and learn how to deal with fear and worry:

1. Acknowledge and embrace your fear completely. Fear grips everyone. You can welcome your feelings as a buddy who teaches you about yourself if you are totally present and honest.

2. Switch from a right/wrong mindset to a can't-lose one. There will be positive consequences regardless of your choice. You might or might not be able to achieve your intended outcome. You haven't failed in any way. You've discovered your abilities and gained a better understanding of your strengths and weaknesses. After some thought, you'll see what you can do to improve your talents and excel.

3. Recognize the advantages of confronting your fear. Avoiding, fleeing, or hiding simply serves to exacerbate your concerns. You'll strengthen your bonds with family and friends as you gain confidence and put yourself out there. You'll be collaborating with coworkers and clients to pinpoint solutions. You're going to be genuine to yourself. Those who care about you will accept you as you are. Those who have a problem with your honesty shouldn't be in your life in the first place.

4. Recognize any fears you may have inherited. Not everyone has parents who inculcate in them the conviction that they can accomplish and be anything they wish. Some of the concerns that arise from your upbringing are fears that surround money, sex, and self-worth.

5. Determine the source of your fear. It's possible that what you say you're afraid of isn't exactly what you're afraid of. If you're frightened of public speaking, for example, you might actually be afraid of rejection, feeling silly, or failing. You can focus on resolving the underlying issues once you've identified them.

6. Rejoice in your progress. Remember each time you've been challenged and pushed yourself beyond your comfort zone. It's important to remember that it's not about winning or losing. It's the way you dealt with it!

7. Avoid making comparisons, as they will only make you feel inadequate. You have a one-of-a-kind set of life experiences. Own your feelings and don't worry about what others might do in your position.

8. Recognize fear as a warning system designed to protect you from real risks. Fearless doesn't imply irresponsibility. Life is fragile, and in times of peril, we must take appropriate safeguards.

9. If you're feeling overwhelmed, start small. Jumping into the deep end of the pool won't help you overcome your fear of swimming. Gradually introducing yourself to the water and having pleasant experiences will help you gain

confidence and a sense of control. Having a mentor to help you get through the stumbling blocks is often necessary.

10. Find a group of people who can help you. When you can express your anxieties to someone you trust, the pressure is relieved, and the problem may turn out to be smaller than you thought. They know you well, and their constructive criticism and encouragement can help you regain your confidence.

Advantages of Being Fearless

People that follow this attitude are referred to as "fearless" or "crazy." However, there are some significant advantages to being brave that exceed the disadvantages.

First, there is a distinction to be made between being confident and being fearless. They're linked, but they're different.

You can go about your day without worrying about rejection or failure if you have confidence. It's a wonderful quality to possess, but fearlessness is the next step up from confidence. You have the guts to take enormous leaps into the unknown when you combine fearlessness and confidence. You can follow your ambitions, construct bridges to places you can't see, and take risks that others wouldn't consider.

Sure, if you fail in your next venture, the pain will be excruciating. But what happens if you succeed? Oh, the benefits!

Yes, there are numerous advantages to being fearless. Here are seven advantages that fearless people enjoy:

1. They acknowledge and accept fear for what it is.
They recognize fear for what it is: the body's concern for their safety. The "fearless" take that dread into consideration, alter their actions as necessary, and move on.

If your safety is actually in jeopardy and you're unable to take precautionary measures, you are unlikely to carry out the plan. If it's a fight-or-flight situation, you'll push through the difficult parts for the thrill of glory on the other side.

2. They're always growing.
It's only when you venture beyond your comfort zone that you can progress. Motivational speakers routinely explore and discuss this subject. Entrepreneurial articles go into great detail about it.

Life is designed to be experienced rather than memorized. Ruts are what they're called by definition.

A fearless person's responsibility is to step out of their comfort zone and into completely new, undiscovered territory. As a result, these individuals are continually learning and improving.

3. They are unfazed by rejection.
It's simpler to do anything in life once you've overcome your fear of rejection.

The phrase "What would people think?" kills most of our dreams. You can focus on achieving your objectives and goals if the ideas and opinions of complete strangers don't bother you. Fearless people recognize that in order to achieve great things, they must face rejection.

4. They're aware of their own existence.
Being "fearless" doesn't truly mean that you're devoid of all fear. It implies that you are capable of analyzing any challenge that comes your way.

You begin to scrutinize yourself as you think through challenges. What is the source of your apprehension? Is it a result of previous experiences or the possibility of negative consequences? Is it biologically programmed for you to feel that fear?

You can overcome any mental challenge once you dive deep and recognize your concerns.

5. It's simple to ask for help.
You may not realize it, but many individuals find it difficult to ask for help. They're concerned about annoying the other person or being turned down.

Turning to someone else for help is second nature to a fearless individual. They are unconcerned about it since they understand that it is an inevitable aspect of life.

We can't do everything on our own, and any task is made easier when two or more individuals work together.

6. They aren't remorseful for what they haven't done.
Regret is excruciating, especially when it comes to missed chances. Nobody wants to lie awake at night regretting the opportunities they didn't take.

This cliché question is commonly asked: *Will you be content with the decisions you made or regret the ones you didn't make when you're on your deathbed?*

You'll never look back and wonder what could have been if you take those chances.

7. However, they do have a lot of stories to tell.
In most cases, bold people have the best stories later in life. They did something brave, and whether it worked out or not, they lived to tell the tale.

This gives them fodder for a story about the time they tried something insane that no one else thought would work or the moment they threw their hands up in the air and took a chance, knowing that failure would mean agony or sadness.

Almost every film is built on the notion that someone will act bravely at some point. Whether it's risking everything to obtain the girl or facing the bad guy to save the world, the film requires bold action. The film would be drab and worthless without it.

Consider things through the eyes of a fictional character. Remind yourself that the first fifteen seconds of any new experience are the most difficult. Once you've made it through that brief period, you'll be rewarded with an adventure on the other side.

Ways to Boost Your Mental Strength and Fearlessness
Your dreams will be stolen by fear! Mental toughness and fortitude are two crucial behaviors you must cultivate over time in order to attain your objectives.

Surprisingly, 75 percent of our fears never come true! Why spend so much time pondering them? Failure is often our greatest worry; while feeling fear demonstrates that you care, fearing too much can spread like wildfire and derail your entire career.

Being in sync with your mind and emotionally secure doesn't happen immediately, but it may be greatly enhanced over time.

The same way you work out to improve your physical strength, you may do the same to improve your mental strength. It's a step-by-step procedure that involves mental exercise. Check out the suggestions below to help you become mentally stronger.

Here are nine things you can start doing today to improve your mental strength and develop a strong mind so you can navigate complex and difficult situations.

1. Be in Control of Your Emotions

The outcome is frequently determined by your prevailing thinking!

That is, if you believe you will fail, you have already convinced yourself that you will. Instead, tell yourself, "I will do this!" to avoid succumbing to negativity. It's via the power of positive thinking that you will have the highest chance of succeeding in life. Don't worry; re-framing your thinking with this technique takes some time, but with practice, you'll be able to shift your perspective from negative to positive.

How we act or react to unpleasant events is heavily influenced by our emotions. As a result, it's critical to recognize and comprehend your sentiments, as well as how they influence our decisions.

What are the benefits of internalizing thoughts? Emotional awareness aids in the avoidance of illogical decisions based on emotions.

2. Make New Objectives

New objectives allow for new achievements.

People cope with negative emotions in a variety of ways, including anger, outbursts, anxiety, and melancholy, but these usual coping tactics will only make them feel better for a short time—frequently inviting with long-term consequences.

Begin by assessing your abilities and devising a long-term strategy for avoiding or regulating these feelings without jeopardizing your health or relationships. How?

Physical movement, such as jogging, dancing, hiking, drawing, or engaging in any other exciting activity, may be the most effective way to divert your mind from the problem at hand. What are some of the ways that exercise can help you become mentally stronger?

Regular weekly exercise has been shown to:
- Reduce stress.
- Boost your self-confidence.
- Improve your sleeping habits.
- Protect yourself against anxiety and depression.

Weekly activity releases endorphins, which interact with pain receptors in the brain to diminish pain perception and experience.

In summary, neurotransmitters such as dopamine and serotonin cause a happy emotion and reaction in the body, resulting in a significant shift in our mindset. If you train modestly for a month, you will notice the results!

3. Keep a List to Ensures Accountability

Experiment with more action and less theory. It's time to get the ball rolling!

Old habits die hard for most of us, but if your desire to change is strong enough, you will succeed. Writing out your short-term goals is a fantastic place to start when it comes to being mentally stronger. Why? It brings them to life and holds you accountable. It's no longer a lie you're telling yourself.

Being dedicated to your objective won't only help you achieve it, but it will also build up your mental power over time. This will allow you to:

- Forge new connections.
- Get rid of outdated behaviors.
- Devise more efficient techniques of operation.

4. Prioritize Living with Joy

When you're joyful, you feel mentally stronger. It's time to reclaim control of your happiness. Avoid making concessions in order to impress others at the expense of pursuing your dreams.

Fear of disappointing others may be holding you back, so concentrate on your own personal goals and gain the fortitude to make decisions that benefit you without offending others.

5. Accept That Profit Comes with Risk

You can only grow as a person if you are willing to take risks.

Taking chances to progress to the next level in your life and seizing the opportunity is what your challenge is all about, whether it's quitting your current work to start your own business or breaking harmful relationships.

Breaking into new territory and accomplishing new goals necessitates taking risks that were previously unthinkable.

6. Know That Everyone Makes Mistakes

Making a mistake isn't the same as failing. Failure is when you don't learn from your mistakes. How can any of us progress if we don't make mistakes? It's natural to be hesitant to try anything new due to a previous failure, yet failing and trying again is necessary for growth.

Instead of being afraid of making a mistake, learn something new from your mistakes and apply what you've learned to make better judgments in the future.

7. Embrace Small Victories

Simple victories in life make us feel good, and we become mentally stronger as a result of those feelings. If you decide to start running one morning, instead of starting with five miles per day, start with five miles each week and set a goal you know you can achieve.

Put tiny goals for yourself that you can achieve; the idea is to set yourself up for success rather than failure. Simple victories make us feel good, and when we feel good, we feel mentally stronger.

8. Put Your History Behind You

Because energy is so important, focus your thoughts on what will help you be more productive. Dwelling on your past failures or successes may prevent you from accomplishing your objectives. Regardless of your history, you must put it behind you and focus your time and attention on your current goal.

9. Choose to Reflect or Celebrate

We have the option of celebrating our achievements or pondering why we are failing. Perhaps the secret is to strike a healthy balance. Frustration and negative thoughts can get the best of us at times, but fearless people have a tendency to shift their focus from considering defeat to appreciating victories.

Why is it vital to celebrate victories? Negative thinking depletes our vitality and weakens our mental state. We can move forward with confidence by reminding ourselves of the outstanding job we've done in the past.

A Negative Person vs. A Positive Person

If a negative person tries ten new things and fails at one, he or she will continually focus on why that one failed.

A positive individual will try ten new things, failing in one of them but celebrating the other nine.

It takes time to reprogram your mind, but being aware of negative thinking allows you to contemplate an alternate thought pattern and develop more positive habits in your daily life. You have the ability to make yourself feel worse or better, so choose the latter option more frequently.

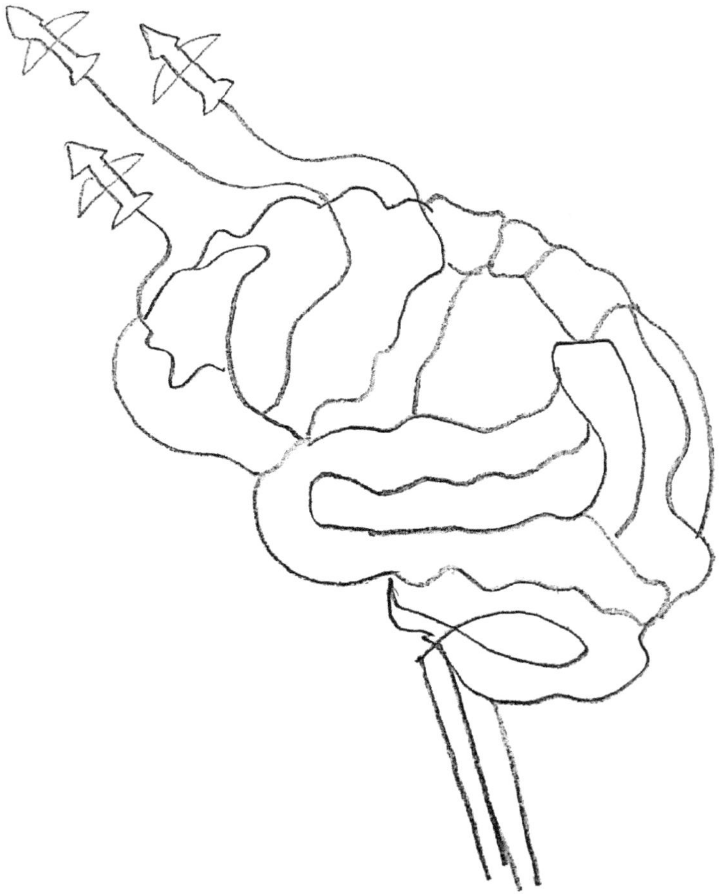

My-mindguide.com

RESILIENCE WITH A FEARLESS MIND

What is the definition of *resiliency*? The ability to adapt to challenging events, retain your well-being in the face of adversity, and bounce back from setbacks in your personal or professional life.

Resilience is a taught characteristic—an attitude that people of all ages can adopt to become more effective in their pursuit of daily chores or even greatness.

What Factors Influence People's Resilience?
Adversity doesn't characterize resilient people. Furthermore, they consider pain or difficult circumstances to be a passing phase.

So, what are the fundamental factors that enable athletes, businesspeople, students, and employees to be so resilient? Let's get a little more into this.

To begin, how we respond to adversity will determine the outcomes and following actions. As a result, our actions, attitudes, and mindset all play a significant impact.

Consider these three characteristics that make people more resilient at work.

1. Self-Awareness

Resilient people are aware of their current situation, their emotions, and other people's actions.

This gives individuals the ability to take control of their behaviors and emotional responses to failure.

Resilient people from all areas of life have a positive outlook on the future, they have set objectives for themselves, and they are determined to attain them.

2. Taking Responsibility for the Situation

Accepting loss or, better still, accepting a setback may appear straightforward, but many people react with emotion first (a dark mist descends upon them when they face hardship), which leads to dissatisfaction and, even worse, a negative mindset.

People that show resiliency swiftly accept the circumstance for what it is and focus their thoughts on moving forward instead of looking back. When it comes to understanding resilience, the importance of acceptance cannot be overstated.

We've all done it, but those who constantly look back have a hard time dealing with the challenges of the present.

3. Victim vs. Survivor Mentality

The gatekeepers to becoming more resilient are your attitude and mindset. What exactly does this imply?

Athletes who approach a half-marathon as victims, for example, are prone to reinforce the same negative messages to themselves. The result? They won't attain the level of performance that they had hoped for. Their mindset convinces them that they have no chance of succeeding, and their failure proves a self-fulfilling prophecy.

So, what is the attitude of a survivor?

Regardless of the obstacles and problems they face, a survivor is always figuring out their next move. They are problem solvers who, rather than lingering on the past, focus their efforts on addressing the issue for a positive conclusion.

Because crises and possible setbacks are unavoidable, resilient individuals use a tunnel vision strategy rather than waste time and energy on problems they can't control. This concentration requires time and effort, but many people who are consistent and persistent in changing their mindset and attitude have developed significant resiliency.

What are the Benefits of Resilience in the Workplace and in Life?

In our daily lives, in business, or at work, we will all be in a position of weakness at times. Our personal path will constantly surprise us, forcing us to make decisions that will either make us sink or swim.

Resilience is a taught trait and process that allows us to recover and regain control in the face of adversity. Being resilient allows us to keep the ship afloat, keep things in perspective, and keep moving forward.

Let's take a look at five fundamental arguments for the importance of resilience:

1. It prevents us from becoming overly stressed.
2. It's an effective tool for staying on track with your objectives.

3. It improves your physical health.
4. It enhances your relationships with coworkers, family members, and others around you.
5. You'll have a better probability of being successful.

Mental Strength 4 C's:

1. Maintain Control

This is how much you believe you have influence over your life, including your emotions and sense of meaning. Your self-esteem might be considered the control component. To score high on the control scale, you must be at ease in your own skin and have a strong sense of self.

You have more emotional control, are less prone to expose your emotional state to others, and are less distracted by other people's emotions. Though you score low on the control scale, you may feel as if events happen to you and you have little control or influence over them.

2. Dedication

This is the level to which you can focus and be dependable on your own. To score well on the commitment scale, you must be able to set and achieve goals consistently without becoming distracted. A high level of commitment shows that you're skilled at creating successful routines and habits.

If you score low on the Commitment scale, you may find it challenging to develop and prioritize goals, as well as create successful routines and habits. Other people or competing priorities may also easily distract you.

3. Take up a Challenge

This metric measures how motivated and flexible you are. A high "challenge" score indicates that you are motivated to accomplish your personal best and that you view difficulties, change, and adversity as opportunities rather than threats; you are also likely to be adaptable and flexible. If you score low on this scale, you may perceive change as a danger and avoid unusual or challenging situations for fear of failing.

4. Self-Assurance

This is how confident you are in your ability to be productive and capable; it's your self-confidence and belief in your power to influence others. To score high on the confidence scale, you must feel that you will accomplish tasks effectively and that you can deal with setbacks while maintaining a routine and even reinforcing your determination. Low confidence indicates that you are easily shaken by setbacks and that you don't believe you are capable or have any influence on others.

14 Ways to Increase and Strengthen Resilience

As we've seen, mental resilience is something that can be enhanced throughout one's life, not an aspect of our personality that's predetermined at birth. We'll look at a variety of mental resilience strategies and techniques in the sections below.

1. Acquiring New Skills

Learning new skills can help to generate a sense of mastery and proficiency, both of which can be useful in difficult times, boosting one's self-esteem and problem-solving abilities.

The skills that must be learned will be determined by the individual. Some people, for example, may benefit from increasing cognitive skills like working memory or selective attention, which will help them operate better in everyday situations. Others might gain from competency-based learning.

Picking up new skills in a group setting has the extra benefit of providing social support, which helps to build resilience.

2. Setting Objectives

The ability to set goals, create meaningful steps to reach those goals, and execute all contribute to the development of willpower and mental toughness. Goals can be big or tiny, and they can be about your physical health, emotional well-being, profession, finances, spirituality, or anything else. Goals involving the acquisition of new skills will reap double benefits. Learning to play an instrument or learning a new language are two examples.

According to some studies, setting and working toward goals that are bigger than oneself, such as religious involvement or volunteering for a cause, might help increase resiliency. This may give you a stronger sense of purpose and connection, which can be beneficial through difficult times.

3. Exposure

Controlled exposure is a technique for helping people overcome their concerns by gradually exposing them to anxiety-provoking stimuli. According to research, this can help people become more resilient, especially when it entails learning new skills and creating goals—a threefold advantage.

For example, public speaking is a vital life skill but also a source of anxiety for many people. Those who are terrified of public speaking might set goals for themselves that include controlled exposure in order to improve or acquire this ability. They can start with a tiny audience of one or two people and gradually grow their audience as time goes on.

This type of action plan can be started by the individual alone or constructed with the help of a therapist skilled in cognitive behavioral therapy. Successful attempts can boost self-esteem, autonomy, and mastery, all of which can be useful in difficult situations.

4. Connect the Dots

Our connections to family, friends, and community members can help us to be more resilient. Healthy relationships with individuals who care about you and will listen to your difficulties can help us rediscover hope during challenging times. Similarly, aiding others in their moment of need can be quite beneficial to us and can strengthen our own sense of resilience.

5. Don't Think of Emergencies as Insurmountable Obstacles

We have no control over the external events that occur around us, but we do have power over how we respond to them. There will always be difficulties in life, but it's crucial to see beyond whatever unpleasant position you're in and know that things will change. As you deal with the challenging situation, pay attention to the subtle ways in which you may already be feeling better.

6. Recognize That Change Is an Inevitable Aspect of Life

According to popular belief, the only constant in life is change. Certain ambitions may no longer be viable or attainable as a result of challenging circumstances. Accepting what you can't alter frees you up to concentrate on the things you *do* have control over.

7. Make Progress toward Your Objectives

While it's critical to set long-term, big-picture goals, it's also critical to make sure they're achievable. Creating tiny, concrete steps allows us to achieve our goals and to work toward them on a regular basis, resulting in minor "wins" en route. Every day, try to take one small step closer to your goal.

8. Be Decisive in Your Actions

Rather than avoiding difficulties and stresses and hoping they'll go away on their own, attempt to take decisive action whenever possible.

9. Look for Opportunities to Learn More about Yourself

Tragedies can sometimes lead to significant personal growth and learning. Living through a traumatic experience can boost our self-esteem and feeling of self-worth, improve our bonds, and teach us a lot about ourselves. Many people who have faced adversity have expressed a deeper spirituality and greater respect for life.

10. Develop a Good Self-Perception

Working to improve your self-confidence can help you avoid problems and create resilience. When it comes to problem-solving and trusting your own intuition, having a good picture of oneself is critical.

11. Maintain a Sense of Perspective

When things are bad, keep in mind that things could be a lot worse; try not to exaggerate things. When dealing with tough or painful circumstances, it's beneficial to have a long-term perspective in order to cultivate resilience.

12. Maintain a Positive Attitude

We are less likely to find a solution when we focus on the bad aspects of a problem and remain scared. Maintain a cheerful, upbeat attitude and anticipate a positive conclusion rather than a negative one. Visualization is a technique that can be useful in this regard.

13. Look after Yourself

Self-care is an important method for developing resilience because it keeps your mind and body in good shape so you can deal with unpleasant situations when they arise. Taking care of yourself entails paying attention to your own wants and feelings, as well as engaging in enjoyable and relaxing activities. Physical activity is also an excellent form of self-care.

14. Additional Resilience-Building Strategies May Be Beneficial

Increasing resilience can mean different things to different people. Journaling, gratitude practice, meditation, and other spiritual practices might help some people reclaim their hope and resolve.

Resilience as a Pathway (APA)

According to the American Psychological Association (2014), resilience is defined as the ability to adapt well in the face of adversity, trauma, tragedy, threats, or severe causes of stress, such as family and relationship issues, serious health issues, or employment and financial stressors. To put it another way, "bouncing back" after adversity. Resilience isn't a personality trait that you either have or lack.

It entails taught and formed behaviors, thoughts, and actions in everyone.

According to current research, resilience is typical, not exceptional, and anybody can demonstrate it. According to the American Psychological Association, being resilient doesn't imply that a person is immune to adversity. People who have dealt with hardships and trauma in their lives are more likely to experience significant emotional anguish.

Resilience Factors

Many factors contribute to resilience, but studies show that having supportive relationships both within and outside the family is the most important. Caring, loving relationships that provide encouragement and reassurance aid in the development of a person's resilience.

Additional qualities linked to resilience, according to the APA, include:

- The ability to establish realistic plans and take actionable steps to carry them out.
- A positive self-image and belief in your own abilities and strengths.
- Problem-solving and communication abilities.
- The ability to control and manage intense emotions and urges.

All of these are qualities that people may cultivate on their own.

Resilience-Building Techniques

When it comes to building resilience, each person's strategy will be different. We all react to traumatic and stressful life experiences differently, so what works for one person may not work for another. For example, cultural differences regarding how people communicate their feelings and cope with adversity may be reflected in some differences in how people convey their feelings and deal with adversity.

Taking Advice from the Past

Examining your prior experiences and sources of personal strength can help you figure out which resilience-building techniques will work best for you. The American Psychology Association has provided some leading questions that you might ask yourself about how you've reacted to difficult situations in the past. Investigating the answers to these questions can assist you in formulating future tactics.

Take into account the following:
- What have been the most stressful experiences in my life?
- How have those events affected me in the past?
- Has it ever helped me to think of key persons in my life when I'm feeling down?
- To whom have I turned for help in the aftermath of a traumatic or stressful event?
- In challenging times, what have I learned about myself and my interactions with others?
- Has assisting someone else going through a similar experience been beneficial to me?
- Have I been successful in overcoming challenges, and if so, how?

Maintaining Flexibility

Flexible thinking equates to a resilient attitude. Maintaining flexibility and balance in the face of stressful situations and events is beneficial in the following ways:

- Allow yourself to feel strong emotions, but recognize when you may need to set them aside in order to work well.
- Take action to address your problems and meet the demands of daily life, but know when to take a step back and rest/reenergize yourself.
- Nurture yourself by spending time with loved ones who provide support and encouragement.
- Know when to rely on others and when to rely on yourself.

Where to Look for Assistance

The love and support of family and friends isn't always enough. When you need support from someone outside your group, don't be afraid to ask for it. People frequently find it beneficial to consult:

- *Support groups for self-help and community.* Sharing experiences, feelings, knowledge, and ideas may be a great source of comfort for those who feel alone through difficult times.

- *Books and other printed materials.* Hearing from individuals who have successfully handled difficult situations similar to yours may be inspiring when it comes to establishing a personal plan.

- *Web-based resources.* There is a multitude of resources and information about dealing with trauma and stress on the

Internet; just make sure the information is from a reliable source.

- *A mental health professional with a license.* For many people, the preceding advice may be adequate to build resilience, but if you're unable to function in your everyday life as a result of traumatic or other stressful life experiences, it's sometimes best to seek professional support.

Keep Your Adventure Going

A useful metaphor for resilience is a kayak journey, which neatly conveys the APA's essential principles. On a rafting excursion, you can expect to encounter a variety of conditions, including rapids, slow water, shallow water, and a variety of crazy turns.

Changes in circumstances affect your ideas, attitude, and how you navigate yourself, just as they do in reality. It helps to have previous experience and information to draw on in life, much as it does when traveling down a river. A strategy that is likely to work successfully for you should guide your journey.

Confidence and a firm belief in your abilities to handle the sometimes-choppy seas, as well as having trusted partners to accompany and encourage you on the journey, are all key factors.

Improving Mental Stability and Resilience

Mental stamina is the single defining characteristic that allows us to persevere in the face of adversity. It's necessary for overcoming long-term obstacles as well as unforeseeable and unexpected struggles, anxieties, or trauma, and it can only be acquired via practice and repetition.

When we talk about strength, we usually think of elite athletes and sports teams because they require both physical and mental stamina to perform well. Increased mental stamina, however, is beneficial to everyone, not just athletes. Although no one develops mental fortitude overnight, the following five suggestions for developing mental fortitude over time may be of great use to you:

1. Keep a Positive Mindset

One of the most crucial features of a healthy mind is self-confidence and belief in one's ability to perform and make decisions. Training yourself to think positively and look for the good in every situation can undoubtedly aid in the development of mental strength over time.

2. Make Use of Visualization Techniques

Visualization is a powerful strategy for dealing with stress and performance anxiety. Close your eyes and recall a time when you overcame a comparable challenge. This involves not just the aesthetic aspect of the success but the emotional one.

3. Be Prepared for Setbacks

Life doesn't always turn out the way we had anticipated or planned. As such, instead of concentrating on the loss or tragedy, it's critical to re-center oneself and regain concentration after a setback. We have no control over the external events that occur in our lives, but we do have power over what we do afterward. It's a good idea to have a strategy in place to assist you in dealing with things that don't go as planned.

4. Dealing with Stress

Our ability to manage stress has a significant impact on our mental power. Although not all stress is negative—positive stress (excitement) can be inspiring—it all has the same physical impact on our bodies.

Meditation and gradual muscle relaxation are two effective stress management approaches. It's critical to remember that you are in charge of your mental state and how you will respond to the stressor.

5. Increase Your Sleep Time

It's no secret that getting enough sleep is essential for our physical and emotional well-being. A good night's sleep will keep you healthy and sharp, capable of making quick decisions. Seven to nine hours of sleep is considered adequate—or more if you engage in high-stress activities, both physical and mental.

Enhancing Community Resilience

Community resilience refers to a community's ability to adapt to, tolerate, and recover from bad conditions by utilizing available resources (energy, communication, transportation, food, and so on).

After a disaster, successful adaptation guarantees that a community can return to normal life as quickly as feasible. The health, functionality, and quality of life of the people are all important factors in community adaptation.

In order to come together and rebuild after a disaster, a community should follow a plan of action, just as it does when faced with any challenge. The following are the essential elements for a community to create collective resilience following a tragedy:

- Boost and protect social support
- Reduce risk and resource disparities
- Engage locals in mitigation
- Create organizational links

Prepare for the possibility of not having a plan, which necessitates adaptability, decision-making skills, and reliable information sources that can work in the face of uncertainty.

What Makes a Relationship Resilient?

Any relationship requires a high level of resiliency. Relationships demand constant attention and nurturing, especially during difficult times. Have you ever pondered why some friendships and sexual relationships seem to last longer than others? Everly (2018) proposes a number of characteristics that appear to encourage resiliency in relationships and increase their chances of survival.

Relationships with High Resilience Have These Characteristics

1. Active Optimism

Active optimism isn't just expecting that things will turn out well; it's about believing that things will turn out well and then taking steps to ensure that they do. In a relationship, this entails agreeing to refrain from making critical, cruel, or cynical remarks in order to harness the power of a positive self-fulfilling prophecy.

2. Honesty, Integrity, Acceptance of Responsibility for One's Actions, and Forgiveness

We're bound to create resilience in our relationships if we commit to taking responsibility for our acts, being loyal to one another, and forgiving one another (and ourselves). This contains the classic adage that, regardless of the outcome or consequences, honesty is the best policy.

3. Determination

This entails having the courage to act, even if it's unpopular or causes conflict in a relationship. Taking decisive action can mean leaving a toxic relationship, and it can also mean promoting one's own personal resilience.

4. Perseverance

The ability to persevere in the face of adversity, setbacks, and failures is referred to as tenacity. In partnerships, it's critical to understand that there will always be ebbs and flows, good and bad times.

5. Self-Discipline

The capacity to regulate impulses, resist temptations, and defer gratification are all vital traits in a relationship. Self-control allows one to avoid behaviors that harm their relationship while supporting positive behaviors, especially when faced with hardship.

6. Honest Communication Promotes Interpersonal Connectivity

Through open, honest communication, a relationship's sense of "belonging" and closeness is maintained and honed. The most difficult talks to conduct are frequently the most crucial.

7. Mindfulness

Present-mindedness offers numerous benefits for individuals, and this is also true for couples in a relationship. Within a partnership, present-minded awareness leads to a peaceful, non-judgmental thinking style and open communication. Rather than dismissing fresh ideas and assigning blame, presence of mind allows for collaborative thought and openness to new solutions.

These are only a few of the traits that predict relationship resilience and boost the likelihood of a relationship rebounding from adversity.

How Do People Learn to Be Resilient for the Rest of their Lives?

It's essential to start strengthening your resilience now if you want to be resilient for the rest of your life! Practice and dedication to the tactics and tips outlined above will improve your capacity to bounce back and adapt, as life *will* throw you some curveballs.

The silver lining to adversity in life is that the more you can flex your resiliency muscle, the stronger it will be!

While resilience-building processes often take years, they can be accelerated by changes or crises; and while some parts of resilience are built into normal settings, most of them are only tested in crisis scenarios.

Despite the fact that each person develops their own coping style, the proposed multi-dimensional resilience model refers to the following six variables that make up each style:

- Values and beliefs
- Affect

- Social
- Imagination
- Cognition
- Physiology

How to Develop a Mind that is Better, Stronger, and More Confident

Recall that one of the four Cs of mental toughness is confidence!

One of the most important aspects of growing resiliency is cultivating a good self-image and gaining confidence in your abilities to solve difficulties and trust your intuition. So, how do we develop a more self-assured mindset?

Here are some solid techniques to start boosting your self-esteem:

1. Get Stuff Done

Confidence and achievement are inextricably linked. Setting and achieving objectives—even tiny steps toward them—can boost your self-esteem and confidence in your talents.

2. Keep Track of Your Progress

It's critical to break down a large or small objective into smaller, more doable steps when working toward it. As a result, it will be easier to track development and build confidence because the progress will be visible in real-time. It aids in quantifying your objectives as well as the steps necessary to achieve them.

3. Act in the Best Interests of Others

Highly confident people are more likely to live by a set of values and make decisions based on those values, even if it isn't always in their best interest. It can build a more confident attitude when your decisions are in line with your highest self.

4. Exercise

Exercise benefits not only your physical body but also your thoughts. Improved focus, memory retention, and stress and anxiety management are all mental benefits of exercise. Exercise has also been linked to the prevention and treatment of depression. Exercise gives you confidence not just because of the physical benefits, but also because of the mental benefits.

5. Have No Fear

Fearlessness in the pursuit of your objectives and goals necessitates a high level of self-assurance. On the other hand, challenging yourself by diving headfirst into situations that worry you might help you gain confidence. It's natural to become overwhelmed and frightened of failure when we set lofty objectives for ourselves. In these situations, it's critical to summon your courage and simply keep moving forward, one step at a time.

6. Take a Stand for Yourself

Standing up for yourself when someone says that you can't do something is a great approach to boost your self-esteem. All too frequently, we believe the critics because they are mirroring the self-doubt we are experiencing in our thoughts. Replacing negative ideas with positive ones is one way to cultivate a positive self-image. When someone doesn't believe in you, try to do the same.

7. Be Consistent

Following through on your promises not only helps you earn the respect of others, but it also helps you gain respect for and confidence in yourself. Develop your follow-through abilities to help you achieve your goals and, more importantly, to strengthen your relationships.

8. Consider the Long Term

We frequently sacrifice long-term enjoyment for momentary gratification. We can gain confidence by making sacrifices and actions that are based on long-term goals rather than immediate gratification. Finding the discipline to do so will bring you more happiness in the long run, as well as a better chance of completing your goals.

9. Don't Give a Damn What Others Think

It's easy to get caught up worrying about what others think of you, but it's crucial to realize that what people think of you has no bearing on your ability to achieve your goals. Build your self-assurance by believing in yourself and continuing to move forward, even if others disagree.

10. Increase the Amount of Time You Spend Doing Things That Make You Happy

It helps to enhance our lives and become our best selves when we take time for self-care and doing the things that offer us joy. When we are aligned with our highest selves and proud of it, we gain confidence.

My-mindguide.com

THINKING OF COVID-19 WITH A FEARLESS MIND

For many of us, these are trying and perplexing times. Fear and anxiety can be overwhelming, causing people to experience powerful emotions. Everyone's daily routine has been severely interrupted around the world. People are concerned about what might occur in the next weeks, months, and years. Anxiety, uncertainty, and worry are all too common nowadays. People are concerned about their own and their loved ones' health. Under the current circumstances, how can we deal with all of our fears? Let's start with the basics:

What Is the Source of Our Apprehension?
Fear is a reaction to uncertainty and the unknown. When we have doubts about how things will end up, fear enters the picture. We're afraid of making a mistake or a bad decision when we doubt ourselves. When we're unsure about the outcome, we're afraid of the implications. We live in terror of chance occurrences and accidents if we doubt the presence of governing force.

We're afraid of becoming weak. The bully is feared by the little boy or girl on the school playground. The weak child fears being physically attacked by the stronger children every day as he or she travels home from school. At work, the employee is afraid of his or her boss. In the hands of our employer, our wage and job security are in jeopardy. We may feel helpless and powerless to speak up about workplace injustices because individuals in positions of authority may react and penalize us.

We're more terrified of what we think is out there than what's *actually* out there. Those who are afraid of death are actually afraid of the unknown. Fear is constantly attempting to devour us alive in one way or another. People are afraid of the unknown because they believe it will be unpleasant or painful. They develop worry and fear because they have no idea what to expect.

How Can We Overcome Our Fears?
Our soul, which is fully aware, is a part of God and, as such, is fearless. It is God in a microcosm because God is all-consciousness and the soul is one with the Lord. God is fearless, and the soul is fearless as well. It's only when we lose contact with our soul that we become terrified. The soul is absolute awareness; the soul is truth. There is no fear when you are connected to the ultimate truth. As a result, the soul is free of dread.

Wisdom is a property of the soul that grants it access to all knowledge. There is nothing that the soul could possibly be unaware of. It understands what is and what will be. What is there to be afraid of? It's been experienced by saints, mystics, prophets, and enlightened people who have been in touch with their souls.

Desensitization is the process of being desensitized to something.

To desensitize someone, a little dosage of the drug to which they are allergic is given. The body gains tolerance to the irritating material by learning to accept little doses and can then handle greater levels over time. We can improve our ability to handle more and greater obstacles if we start practicing fearlessness in little situations. We must connect with our empowered spirit in order to exercise fearlessness.

How Can We Feel Our Soul's Power and Fearlessness?

We must understand that it's our empowered soul that is actually facing our issues. We shall transcend all fears and obtain a lasting sense of serenity and security if we connect with our empowered spirit. Our enlightened soul, which is one with God, is always there for us. It's there to assist us in overcoming life's difficulties. All we have to do now is sit in solitude and feel our powerful soul.

Meditation is a technique for diverting our attention from the outside world and back to ourselves. We disconnect from the chaos of our environment and reconnect with our soul, which is a part of God, the source of all love and joy.

What Can We Do Now, Given the Circumstances?

Life's difficulties are unavoidable. We have no power over the universe beyond our own. We can't guarantee that we won't lose our job, our house, our fortune, or a loved one. What we *can* do is approach these issues with a spirit of fearlessness, so that dread and despair don't paralyze us. What we *can* do is spend time in meditation, feeling our powerful soul instead of reading, viewing, or listening to news articles, including social media.

Our life will be filled with love, joy, fearlessness, acceptance, and trust once we become conscious of our spiritual essence and feel our soul.

These six suggestions may be useful:

1. *Reassure Yourself That It Will Get Better* – Most people's anxiety will subside as the COVID-19 threat fades. Anxiety can be addressed if it doesn't go away.

2. *Alter Your "Information Diet"* – Reading harrowing accounts of COVID-19's tragedies is more likely to aggravate anxiety than to decrease it. Instead, try focusing on positive facts, stories, or activities to divert your attention from your anxieties.

3. *Consider the Risk Logically* – Coronavirus has caused tragedy in many families, and we recognize that the risk and consequences of catching the virus vary from person to person. Keep in mind that in Australia, over 90 percent of persons who have been infected with the coronavirus have recovered. The number of infections is also still quite low, with only 7,072 confirmed cases out of a population of over twenty-five million people.

4. *Reduce Your Body's Focus* – Paying too much attention to our bodies might cause us to notice things we wouldn't typically notice, leading to increased anxiety. Focusing on other things, such as pleasant, fun hobbies, might help you take your mind off your body.

5. *Go Slowly and at Your Own Pace* – It's fine to ease back into doing activities you used to do. Take it one step at a time,

one activity at a time, so you may feel safe while gradually increasing your confidence.

6. *Put Your Anxiety into Action* – Focusing on what you can control will help. Taking active actions to maintain your mental health, such as sleeping properly, exercising, engaging in entertaining or soothing activities, and remaining socially connected, can make a huge difference.

ECO-ANXIETY

We've long since moved past dismissing evidence of climate change as just another stage in the natural cycle of global warming and cooling. Human actions have changed the Earth's climate, and the consequences are becoming increasingly obvious.

Most individuals are aware that climate change can harm physical health via pollution, the spread of disease, and food scarcity. One severe mental health effect, according to mental health practitioners, is eco-anxiety.

Anxiety regarding the future of the Earth and the life it shelters is referred to as eco-anxiety.

Is This Normal?
When your body perceives a threat, it responds with the fight-flight-freeze survival mechanism. We frequently consider these perceived threats to be based on illogical anxieties.

However, climate change is a serious concern, no matter how far off the end result appears to be. In this light, eco-anxiety could be viewed as a rare instance of anxiety acting as it should. It serves as a survival motive, eliciting a distinct emotional reaction that drives humanity to seek solutions to climate change.

How Does It Feel?

If you're concerned about irreversible changes in temperature, weather, and animal and human ecosystems, you're not alone. Perhaps you, like many others, are emotionally traumatized by the damage that has already been done to certain natural ecosystems and species.

One manifestation of eco-anxiety is a growing sense of helplessness as it relates to the planet's changes. Symptoms include:

- Fatalistic thinking
- Existential dread
- Guilt or shame about your own carbon footprint
- Post-traumatic stress after experiencing climate change's effects
- Feelings of depression, anxiety, or panic
- Grief and sadness over the loss of natural environments or wildlife populations
- Obsessive-compulsive disorder

These feelings can contribute to secondary issues, like:
- Sleep problems
- Appetite changes
- Difficulty concentrating

Stress can put a severe strain on friendships, sexual relationships, and familial interactions, especially if you don't share the same views on climate change.

Concerns about climate change may become so overpowering that you seek distractions to alleviate your anxiety. Distracting yourself, however, may not be helpful if it prevents you from working through your emotions or involves less-than-ideal coping mechanisms, such as substance or alcohol abuse.

Where Does It Originate?

Climate change is a worldwide issue, but it also affects individuals. Even if you don't spend much time thinking about your relationship to the earth, it exists for everyone.

You've probably heard of Mother Earth, and there's some truth to it. Earth is the first home and the first source of resources.

Even if you feel disconnected from this world, you wouldn't exist if it weren't for Earth. It's only normal to be sad as you watch the world change so quickly.

Here are some of the other variables that contribute to eco-anxiety.

Experiential Learning

It's one thing to hear about climate change's long-term consequences and quite another to go through them.

Perhaps hurricanes or wildfires forced you to flee your home or completely destroyed it. Perhaps you've lost loved ones in similar calamities—lives that, unlike homes, are irreplaceable. Gradual effects, such as excessive heat and increasing rainfall, may go unnoticed at first, but don't underestimate their importance. They can nevertheless have an impact on you in the following ways:

- High temperatures can cause a variety of problems, including increased stress and irritation.

- People taking psychiatric drugs that impact body temperature regulation can be heavily impacted. Less sun implies more rain (or dense, smoky air, depending on where you are). Sunlight encourages the creation of serotonin, a hormone related to decreased anxiety and despair, as well as improved general health. You're more likely to experience mood-related symptoms, such as seasonal depression, if you don't get enough sunlight.

Broadening the Scope of News Coverage

On the one hand, more media coverage of climate change is a sign of progress, as increased awareness can lead to more people taking action.

However, doom-scrolling and the inability to avoid hearing about climate change may not necessarily encourage change. The constant flood of news about dwindling rainforests, coral reef devastation, and species dwindling to single digits might exacerbate your shock and anguish.

In certain circumstances, intense despair can make it impossible to begin taking any action at all.

Regretting Your Own Influence

It's easy to pass severe judgment on yourself for lifestyle choices that contribute to climate change. Using plastic and Styrofoam, operating your air conditioner, and eating a meat-heavy diet are all examples of bad habits.

Feelings of regret and shame for your actions may coexist with feelings of powerlessness, fueled by the fact that you only have so much time to make a difference. While you can take actions to lessen your carbon footprint, no one person can address climate change on their own. It's a large-scale issue that necessitates a worldwide commitment to radical change.

As a result, your individual efforts may appear to be a drop in a big bucket. Anxiety about the environment may, thus, be exacerbated by a sense of powerlessness.

Who Is the Most Vulnerable?

Because everyone is reliant on the planet's health, eco-anxiety can impact anyone. Certain groups, on the other hand, are more vulnerable to climate change and thus face a larger risk of suffering as a result of it.

The following groups are particularly vulnerable:
- Indigenous peoples
- Those who live on islands, in coastal or desert areas, or in other geologically hazardous areas
- Communities that are socioeconomically disadvantaged
- Elderly adults and children
- Persons with disabilities or long-term health issues

A number of complex elements play a role in increased risk:

- Families with a lower annual income may find it more difficult to cope with the effects of a natural disaster, which is likely to exacerbate sadness and distress.

- Native Alaskans, Inuit tribes, and other Indigenous peoples whose lives are centered on sea ice and other shifting climates are at risk of losing not only their way of life but also their cultural and personal identities.

- Fishing, hunting, and agricultural communities are at risk of losing their land, income, and way of life. Long periods of drought are linked to a greater prevalence of suicide among farmers.

- Many tourist sites are impacted heavily due to their gorgeous natural surroundings. The alteration and destruction of these settings is certain unless significant counter-measures are taken. When such destinations *are* ultimately destroyed, decreasing tourist numbers can damage the local economy.

Furthermore, many of the groups at the greatest risk face greater hurdles to medical and mental health care. Because they don't have access, they can't get the help they need to deal with climate-related stress.

How Do You Handle It?
Despite the fact that climate change may appear to be an impossibly large concern, you may still take steps to safeguard your mental health.

Examine Your Own Behavior
Adopting "greener" (more sustainable) lifestyle practices can frequently help you grow your sense of self by allowing you to live more in line with your personal ideals.

Furthermore, adopting climate-friendly actions may inspire others to follow suit. This can be accomplished in a variety of ways, including:

- Calculating your carbon footprint will help you see where you can make changes to lessen your impact.

- Choosing physical commuting over driving (e.g., biking or walking) can enhance both your physical and emotional health, all the while lowering carbon emissions.

- You can get involved in broader policy initiatives to address climate change by reaching out to community organizations that are striving to safeguard the environment.

Reject Denial

Climate change is a frightening prospect. It's understandable to try to prevent eco-anxiety by completely shutting out your misery.

However, burying your head in the sand makes it even more difficult to act. It won't make you feel any better, either, because hiding negative feelings usually makes them worse.

It's easier said than done, but these pointers can assist you in staying on track:

- Allow yourself to fully acknowledge your sentiments rather than rejecting the truth of climate change or putting them aside.

- If you're feeling guilty about past actions that weren't environmentally friendly, forgive yourself and resolve to make better choices in the future.

- Compassion for yourself and others is essential. You're only one person, and a single person can only accomplish so much.

- Spend time protecting the beaches, hiking routes, and mountain lakes that you care about. Nature, as endangered as it is, provides medicinal advantages that might help you relax.

Make Friends with Your Neighbors

Participating in community gardening, trash pickup, or waste reduction projects can also help to alleviate emotions of environmental anxiety.

Working with people who are concerned about the environment can help you feel more connected and relieve the feeling of being alone. Emotional and social support can help you increase your optimism and hope by boosting your resilience.

Many voices reverberate louder than a single voice. Efforts to safeguard communal green areas, such as parks, nature preserves, and forests, may have a better chance of succeeding if the community comes together.

Children's Coping Strategies

Children are also affected by environmental anxiety, though younger children may find it difficult to comprehend and process these complex feelings.

As adults hand down a world on the verge of collapse, older children may display concern, if not outright resentment, at the grim view of their future.

These tactics can assist you in coping as a group.

Let's Talk About It

You might be concerned that talking about climate change will make your children feel worse, yet talking about fears can often help to reduce their intensity. Creating a safe area for them to talk about something that could change their lives encourages them to start expressing and dealing with their fears.

Validate their pain and let them know you're experiencing it as well. Pay attention to their inquiries, and provide age-appropriate, fact-based responses. If they ask you a question that you don't know the answer to, instead of offering ambiguous answers, conduct some research.

A more conscious and informed generation results from open, honest dialogue. Children can be empowered by discussing climate change because it gives them a sense of agency to take action on their own.

As a Family, Take Action
A family effort can make a difference for your children, just as committing to ecologically beneficial practices can help you feel less anxious about the environment.

Spend some time thinking about how you might save energy and resources in your home. For instance, you could:

- Choose to cycle or walk to school and work.
- Lower the thermostat a few degrees and dress more warmly indoors.
- Get creative with leftovers to reduce food waste.
- Shop at thrift stores instead of purchasing new items.
- Build a garden in your backyard.
- Encourage everyone's participation and make it a continuous effort once you've developed a family strategy.
- Enjoy nature as a group.

Providing the opportunity for children to experience nature from a young age helps them become more familiar with it.

Children who engage in activities such as woodland bathing, stargazing, or exploring the variety of life found in tide pools and ponds are more likely to acquire a strong desire to protect and restore natural ecosystems. They'll also discover how nature can enhance well-being and emotional health, which can help them avoid environmental anxiety.

What Can Therapy Do for You?
Despite the fact that eco-anxiety isn't a recognized mental health disorder (yet), therapists and other mental health specialists believe that it has a significant emotional impact on many people.

Even efforts to combat climate change might exacerbate discomfort since doing too much can leave you with little energy for self-care.

Therapy can assist if you're having trouble coping with the symptoms of eco-anxiety or feeling worn out from activism or news exposure.

All therapists can provide a safe environment to:
- Develop coping strategies to manage emotional pain by working on self-compassion.

- Get treatment if you're depressed or anxious, and make a self-care strategy that's unique to you.

Ecotherapy is a new approach to mental health treatment that draws on nature's healing powers and emphasizes the necessity of nourishing not just the environment but also your own relationship to the world.

4 Ways to Overcome Your Eco-Anxiety

"The Planet Is Dying." "Global Warming Will Decimate the Globe." "By 2025, the Atmosphere Will Entirely Shift." We all hear these kinds of headlines on a daily basis these days because climate change is a significant issue. However, this discussion, or should we say panic, over climate change has created an eco-anxiety fear in the minds of people, resulting in mass discomfort.

According to a poll done by The Harris Poll on behalf of the American Psychological Association, two-thirds of the world's population is currently concerned about climate change. People are having panic attacks as a result of various climate change news and predictions, which has caused an anxiety pandemic.

Now, if you suffer from environmental anxiety, where you go to bed every night fearing that you might not wake up in the morning or that the climate will significantly change, you should stop fretting and start practicing the following activities.

Amass Information

To get to the bottom of the issue of environmental change, you'll need to gather essential data and information. Most individuals only hear panicked and pessimistic news and turn off other sources of information. People only read the headlines of interesting topics—so hyperbole is common in the media.

Experts advise that if you obtain all necessary facts, such as how the climate is changing and how your tiny efforts can make a big difference in the changing environment, you should do so. Instead of worrying, you'll be able to take action to safeguard the environment after you understand how to prevent the environment from changing.

Discover How to Make a Difference

It's a terrible problem, and most people have no idea how they can help the environment by making improvements. True, the government and authorities will make significant reforms to safeguard the environment, but there are still few tools in the hands of the average person to protect the environment. You can cut carbon emissions by eating less red meat, for example. Furthermore, you'll be able to raise awareness by joining environmental preservation groups and engaging in strikes or protests.

Environmental preservation is a global issue, and we should all do our part to help safeguard it. Within your means, you should take action to combat climate change.

Negative Thoughts Should Be Refocused

Reframing negative beliefs has been shown in studies to help with stress, anxiety, and depression. If you've been putting off making future plans because of bad thoughts about climate change or environmental damage, it's time to refocus your negative thinking. You should strive to replace one negative thought with one positive one. For example, if the notion of climate change makes you feel anxious, you can replace it with a pleasant thought about how lovely your life is.

Consider Other Important Aspects

This is a one-of-a-kind method for treating stress whereby the stress itself is used to *cure* stress. Yes, when you're worried about the environment, you can think about other looming pressures in your life, such as money, your work, your personal life, and so on. So, while you're thinking about other major stressors in your life, the subject of environmental change will naturally fall to the back of your mind. It isn't the most recommended method, but if none of the others work, you can try it as a last resort.

So, if you're worried about the environment, climate, or the world, you're not alone; a lot of other people are as well. To solve your situation, you must be upbeat and begin taking concrete steps to combat climate change.

Climate change-related emotional pain may appear to be less significant than the actual, serious harm that many people are now experiencing around the world.

However, rather than filtering out these feelings, it's critical to pay attention to them. After all, the key to change is awareness. There's just one planet available to us. We won't be able to leave it because we don't have a way out, so we'll have to fight for it instead.

CONCLUSION

It takes time to develop mental strength; it's the outcome of the everyday practice of positive habits. Strong-willed people establish boundaries, respect themselves, and don't expect others to take control of their lives.

Others admire your fearlessness because you have the confidence to take enormous risks. Most people wish they had the courage to make the decisions that would lead them closer to their goals, but they are too concerned with the small print.

When you're fearless, you're willing to take chances. You work hard to achieve your objectives. And you deal with the ramifications, both positive and negative.

It takes a lot of courage to be brave. However, if it were easy, it wouldn't be such a remarkable quality.

If you enjoyed this title and would like to read about other topics that have changed my life, please check out my new books on Amazon or my website: www.my-mindguide.com.

Also, let's stay connected on social media. Please drop a line on Facebook or Instagram, and stay tuned for updates! You're welcome to share your thoughts with me directly as well: gassner@my-mindguide.com. In return, I'll send you a gorgeous infographic that you can cut out and frame.

Also, please leave a review on Amazon, as this will help me to reach an even broader audience. Thank you so much for your time, insight, and undying hunger for knowledge!

I want to say thank you to all of my colleagues, clients, friends, and family members, who have all contributed to what I am now.

I also want to say thank you to Gabriel Palacios, the king of hypnotherapy and a Swiss bestseller author who taught this old fox new tricks, letting me deep-dive into the mystery of hypnotherapy. I learned so much along the journey that I'm now a certified master-hypnosis coach and conversation coach myself!

Furthermore, I want to say thank you to the fantastic teachers of SAMYANA/Bali who trained me to become a certified yoga and meditation teacher.

Last but not least, I give a special thanks to my master-teacher Eckhard Wunderle, who's close to a saint to me. He introduced me to the world of meditation and let me discover all the wonders it has to offer. I couldn't be more proud about having received my certification as a meditation teacher from directly from him at the Institut für Spirituelle Psychologie.

Peace, love, and happiness to all of you—till next time!

FEARLESS MINDSET

The fearless mindset can guide you toward a life free of apprehension. Whether we're talking about common phobias or severe anxiety disorders, the simple steps contained within can teach you to deal with fear in no time, claiming the life you deserve.

Offering up the perfect balance of personal experience and cutting-edge research, *Fearless Mindset* is an invaluable tool for those who wish take a stand against the negative voices that whisper "you can't." Learn to realize your full potential, and set yourself on course for success.

The fearless mindset can help you cope with life's obstacles, gain strength, and even be a better person. Fearless individuals remain optimistic throughout the hardest of times, and the power of positivity is key to prosperity. Daring to dream means taking chances, but risk can stand in the way of reward. So, safeguard your future by supercharging your confidence today!

Author **Kurt Friedrich Gassner** has spent decades deep-diving into the subjects that mean most to him. Now you're poised to benefit from this wealth of truly timeless knowledge. Say goodbye to fear, and be prepared to meet the whole new you

AUTHORS PORTRAIT

Kurt Friedrich Gassner has worn many hats throughout his lifetime, including but not limited to serial entrepreneur, Creative Director, Meditation Teacher, Licensed Hypnotherapist, and more recently, self-improvement author. Leveraging his treasure trove of experiences and in-depth knowledge of psychology, he provides his readers with the tools they need to unlock their infinite potential.

As a prolific self-help writer, Kurt has authored the following books: *The Art of Forgiveness, Lie or Die, Soul-Match, Can You Inherit a Poisoned Mind?* and *The Power of Poverty.* He also authored a best-selling children's book in German-speaking countries and has over 20 books underway.

When it comes to enduring success, Kurt understands that financial prosperity isn't the only aspect one should strive for. He may be a self-made millionaire, but what really transformed his life is mastering his unconscious mind. Perseverance, personal power, self-awareness, and learning from past mistakes have all been key ingredients to bringing his dreams to fruition—and he strives to impart that wisdom onto others through his writing.

During his spare time, Kurt Friedrich Gassner is either traveling across the globe, golfing, biking in the Alps, hiking, or spending quality time with his loved ones. For the last 37 years, he has been happily married and he is the father of two successful children. Presently, he resides in both Munich, Germany, and Kirchberg, Austria.

OTHER BOOKS BY THE AUTHOR

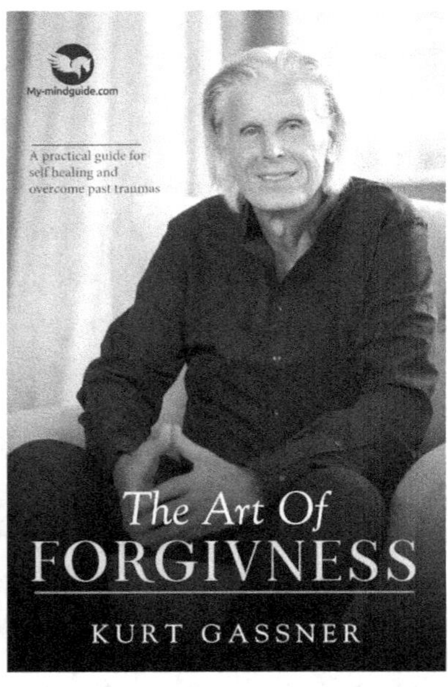

OTHER BOOKS BY THE AUTHOR

OTHER BOOKS BY THE AUTHOR

OTHER BOOKS BY THE AUTHOR

OTHER BOOKS BY THE AUTHOR

BORN
in the
COLD
Liebe und Aufmerksamkeit in der Wachstumsphase eines Kindes
KURT GASSNER

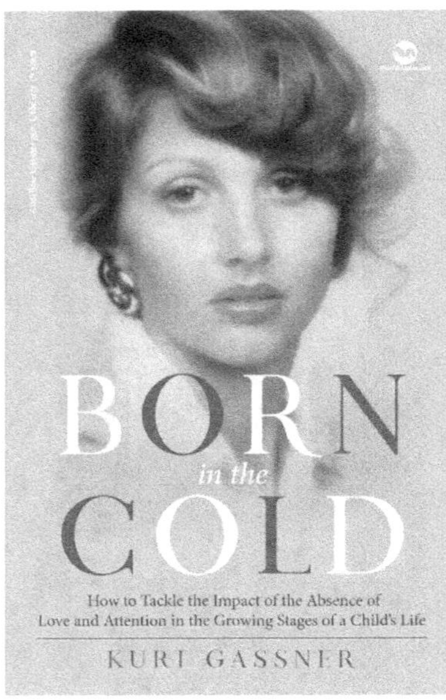

BORN
in the
COLD
How to Tackle the Impact of the Absence of
Love and Attention in the Growing Stages of a Child's Life
KURT GASSNER

SOPHIAS WUNDERWELT
10 ERZÄHLUNGEN
KURT GASSNER

SOPHIA'S WONDERWORLD
10 TALES
KURT GASSNER

BESTSELLING AUTHOR OF
The Art Of
FORGIVNESS
AMAZON #1 BESTSELLER
My-mindguide.com
A practical guide for self-healing and overcome past traumas
The Art Of
FORGIVNESS
KURT GASSNER
The Art Of
FORGIVNESS
KURT GASSNER

9 783987 939228